Lift High the Cross

Lift High the Cross

Choosing the Way of the Cross

Robert C. Morgan

Abingdon Press
Nashville

LIFT HIGH THE CROSS

Copyright © 1995 by Abingdon Press

Library of Congress Cataloging-in-Publication Data

Morgan, Robert C., 1933-
    Lift high the cross / Robert C. Morgan.
        p.   cm.
    ISBN 0-687-21851-9 (alk. paper)
        1. Jesus Christ—Devotional literature.   2. Jesus Christ—
Crucifixion.   3. Crosses.   I. Title.
BT453.M83 1995   94-40486
232.96—dc20   CIP

Scripture quotations unless otherwise indicated are from the New Revised Standard Version Bible, copyright © 1989, by the Division of Christian Education of the National Council of the Churches of Christ in the United States of America and are used by permission.

Scripture quotations noted NEB are from The New English Bible. © The Delegates of the Oxford University Press and The Syndics of the Cambridge University Press 1961, 1970. Reprinted by permission.

Scripture quotations noted KJV are from the King James Version of the Bible.

The excerpt from NIGHT by Elie Wiesel, Copyright © 1960 by MacGibbon & Kee and copyright renewed © 1988 by The Collins Publishing Group. Reprinted by permission of Hill and Wang, a division of Farrar, Straus & Giroux, Inc.

95 96 97 98 99 00 01 02 03 04—10 9 8 7 6 5 4 3 2 1

MANUFACTURED IN THE UNITED STATES OF AMERICA

To Martha,
who constantly inspires me
to lift high the cross

Contents

Introduction

Paul wrote to the Corinthians, "The message about the cross is foolishness to those who are perishing." But, "God's foolishness is wiser than human wisdom" (I Corinthians 1:18, 25). Countless persons throughout history, who have paused long enough to consider the meaning of the cross, have found light for the dark places of life, hope for a different world, healing for their brokenness, and strength for their daily struggle.

Too often we look at the cross only from the human side and see it in terms of the forces that made it. There is also the other side of the cross: God's side. It is from the vantage of the one who was crucified that we can begin to understand why the cross is central to the Christian gospel.

From the standpoint of God's side of the cross, the nature of God begins to come clear. If there could exist in Jesus Christ a love that would go as far as the cross, then surely it must be so with God. In other words in the ultimate nature of things—in the height of the universe or the depth of our being—there is a love that will never let us go.

Jürgen Moltmann, in *The Crucified God*, declares the cross is the clue to all human existence. It is the clue especially to what he calls the "double crisis" that plagues the church today, namely, the question of relevance and the crisis of identity. Moltmann's point is important for us. It is in grasping the hard truth of the cross—its suffering, pain, and rejections—that we come to understand clearly our Christian identity. It is living in solidarity with the crucified Christ that creates relevance.

Christ died on the cross not simply to inspire us, but to save us. He offered his life not only to move our hearts but also to accomplish God's redemptive will. This is where the cross makes a difference in our lives and the world. We are able to lift high the cross and live as redeemed persons whose failures are overcome by love. We are made members of a community—the church—which is no longer intimidated by fear and death. We go with the crucified Christ, who has brought liberation to the world.

We need to be honest in defining what it means to lift high the cross even if we refuse to do it. It is not a fate endured but a mission undertaken. It is not something we have to bear but something we choose. "No one takes it from me," said Jesus. "I have power to lay it down, and I have power to take it up again." (John 10:18). He was speaking of his life. For Jesus, the cross was not an inescapable burden thrust upon him. He could have escaped the cross. He chose to endure it!

To lift high the cross is to choose the way of Christ in all things and to remain faithful even when it is hard to be faithful. It is to be obedient and faithful in the face of rebuke or rejection or ridicule or sorrow or hardship. It is to do the Christlike thing. We may be called to die for our faith, but in the meantime we are called to reproduce the implications of that cross in every encounter of life.

This book attempts to examine the varied circumstances we face in daily life in the light of the cross. What do Christians do when we are lonely, sorrowful, afraid, grief-stricken, tempted to run or conform? What do we do when it is hard to forgive, to love, to be hopeful? What do we do when God seems hidden and the storms of life are raging all around us? We need to lift high the cross in these and all circumstances as a reminder to do as Christ would do.

To lift high the cross is to commit ourselves to the will of God and never run out on that commitment. In place of comfortable, conventional conformity or complacency, it may require of us a solitary life of courage.

The true crossbearers, those who choose to lift high the cross in daily life, hold the hope of humanity, for they are the true followers. They live out everyday life holding fast to Christ's love, faith, confidence, courage, loyalty, and example.

Lift High the Cross

1

Lift High the Cross

**Read
I Corinthians
1:17-33.**

There is no situation or circumstance in our lives that God does not know and care about. The old hymn "Does Jesus Care?" expresses an affirmation that is vital to our faith. The cross reminds us that God is with us in the ordinary and extraordinary circumstances of our daily lives.

George Kitchin and Michael Newbolt's hymn "Lift High the Cross" exhorts Christians to lift up the cross as a symbol of the love of Jesus. As a symbol of Jesus' sacrificial life, the cross challenges every believer to lift the cross in every circumstance of life and live a Christ-like life. Look at the words:

> Lift high the cross,
> the love of Christ proclaim
> till all the world adore his sacred name.

As Christians, we lift high the cross and carry it into life, remembering what the cross was for Jesus.

There are some things we need to understand about the cross of Jesus when we consider lifting it up in our lives.

THERE ARE THOSE WHO FIND THE CROSS UGLY AND REPULSIVE

I recall a "Service of the Last Seven Words" sponsored by the local minister's fellowship to which I belonged some years ago. The service was scheduled for Good Friday from noon until three o'clock in the afternoon. One of the local pastors protested by saying that his father was a merchant and those were the three best retail hours of the year. He then went on to say that he wasn't sure he wanted to participate because he did not like to talk much about the cross. He concluded by saying, "My denomination finds the cross repulsive."

One Lenten season in Dallas there stood an unusual cross on the lawn of a local church. The cross, which was more than ten feet high, stirred a lot of controversy within the congregation and the city. Pictures of it were carried by newspapers across the country and by many television stations. This ugly cross was made of weapons of crime and violence, most of which had been confiscated by Dallas police. There were guns and pistols and knives and bayonets and bullets and bombs and broken bottles. The cross rose out of the remains of an automobile that had been smashed almost flat in a traffic accident. The base was surrounded by barbed-wire entanglements like those surrounding a prison.

It was not easy to look upon this cross of violence, and many people hated the sight of it. There were petitions to have it removed. There were cries that the ugly cross was a sacrilege and desecration of the cross. One pastor commented, "The reaction was understandable: we do not like to be reminded of the suffering of God for our sin."

We do not like to be reminded of the suffering of God because of the inhumanity of the cross, and so we remove any resemblance of the ugly and cruel cross. We use polished silver or gold with ornate designs, or we fashion crosses of brass for the altar in the church. We make them smooth and sleek. We seem determined to forget that the cross was unsightly. It was a horrible means of execution. It was and is repulsive.

Many people want Easter without Good Friday, never realizing that the joy and brightness of the Resurrection morn cannot be experienced until one experiences the sorrow and the darkness of Good Friday. Many want the joy of the Christian life without understanding that there is a cross at the center of Christianity that needs to be understood and experienced.

During an edition of the ABC network television program, "Good Morning America," cohost Charles Gibson interviewed a jewelry designer. She was marketing a new line of crosses designed by popular rock star Madonna and labeled "The Madonna Cross." Among the things she said in the interview was that "Madonna has brought a new dimension to the cross. Never has wearing the cross been more popular than today."

Gibson challenged the statement by saying he understood the cross to be a Christian symbol. "Not anymore," his guest responded. "It is a fashion statement today. No one wears the cross for religious reasons anymore." Gibson continued to challenge her, but she insisted that the cross was "the trend of the day." Like

Gibson, I wanted to challenge what she was saying, but I had to admit that for many people, the cross is only decorative.

Regardless of our sentimentalism, the crucifixion of our Lord on Golgotha was ugly, and yet the cross of Christ remains central to the gospel and Christian thought, devotion, and experience. It cannot be avoided or ignored.

THERE ARE THOSE WHO FIND THE CROSS REDEMPTIVE

Something in all of us drives us to seek explanation for the deep things of life. From the beginning, believers felt the cross deserved a central place in their faith. It was inevitable that they should begin to construct doctrines of the cross—the atonement. The word *atonement* is best understood as meaning at-one-ment: through the cross, persons are made at one with God. They are redeemed. The atonement may be too great a mystery to be reduced to some neat little explanation. Still, there is something in us that drives us to understand it better, even if we cannot completely explain it.

The cross was repulsive, and yet the early Christians found in it a promise of hope, not despair—a promise of life, not death. They began to understand the cross as a means of reclaiming their fragmented lives. It became the sign of power in the universe that can take tragedy and evil and use them for some greater purpose.

The cross is evidence that God will not give up on us. There is no circumstance we may find ourselves in where God is not present. Just think, God knows all about us and yet believes in us enough to die on a cross for us. God took all that anyone could do to the Almighty and to one another and redeemed it into the highest gift of love.

If in the cross of Christ there was reality in the *reality* struggle and pain and suffering, then this means that Christ really chose to suffer for people like you and me, and he did so knowing all the frailties of human nature and our unworthiness. It was a holy love suffering unjustly, bearing the brunt of sin and responding with love. *Christ atone — humble.*

Paul wrote to the Philippians: "Let the same mind be in you that was in Christ Jesus, who, though he was in the form of God, did not regard equality with God as something to be exploited, but emptied himself, taking the form of a slave, being born in human likeness. And being found in human form, he humbled himself and became obedient to the point of death—even death on a cross" (Philippians 2:5-8).

Jesus died on the cross not simply to inspire us but to give us salvation; he offered his life not only to move our hearts but to accomplish God's redemptive will. *Jesus died for our redemption* This is where the cross makes a difference in our lives and in the world. We are able to live as redeemed persons, as those whose heartaches are overcome by love.

In his novel *The Blood of the Lamb*, Peter De Vries speaks of this gift of love. He tells the story of a man who, as a little boy, lost his faith in God when his younger brother died. He was never quite able to reconcile the loss of his brother with a God of love. Across the years he struggled to regain his faith. One day as a father and as an adult, he was on the verge of reclaiming his lost belief, only to be plummeted into despair when his daughter, his only child, was diagnosed with leukemia. As the months passed he lived between hysteria and hope as he watched his daughter go back and forth between hospital and home. For hours at a time he sat in her room and looked on her emaciated body. The man's faith was again called into question. As he watched her die, the only prayer he could offer to God was a cry for help: "I ask, my Lord, only for permission to despair."

On the day his daughter died, the father walked out of the hospital in a blind rage. As he passed the church next door to the hospital, where he had often visited and tried to pray, he found himself standing before the crucifix outside the church. Holding the birthday cake he had brought for his daughter earlier in the day, a gift she never saw, he took the cake out of the box, balanced it in the palm of his hand, and threw the cake in the face of the crucified Christ where it landed just below the crown of thorns. At that moment he saw a miracle happen: "Then through scalded eyes I seemed to see the hands of the crucified Christ free themselves of the nails and move slowly toward the soiled face. Very slowly, very deliberately, with infinite patience, the icing was wiped away from the eyes and flung away. Then the cheeks were wiped down with the same sense of brave and gentle ritual, with all the sobriety of one whose voice could be heard saying, 'Suffer the little children to come unto me . . . for of such is the kingdom of heaven.'"

De Vries confesses the grieving father was found by God and redeemed at that place, the foot of the cross. Redemption was the only alternative he had to death.

So for us, and for our world, the cross is our only alternative to destruction. It is the key to Christ, to the church, indeed to life. At the cross, the inhumanity of the world and our sin are experienced and forgiven. All sinners are made one with God whose love will never leave us alone.

Jesus' words indicate that the cross is the way that offers redemption to those who follow him. Jesus said, "take up [your] cross daily" (Luke 9:23). These words have been twisted into ridiculous interpretations. Sometimes persons have referred to their various physical maladies or irritating circumstances of daily life as their crosses that they had to bear daily. An auto mechanic reported that a woman customer had a rattle in the dashboard of her new BMW. He said regardless of how hard he tried, he could not repair it. "Oh well," she said, "this is just my cross, and I will have to bear it!" Sometimes persons have referred to the care of their own children as their "burdensome cross to carry." This is sacrilegious nonsense!

In the cross, there is a promise for those who lift it high, that nothing is finished until God is finished with it. To have this assurance in the face of any darkness, whether it is personal or societal, can be a source of strength for us. It is to have the confidence that nothing is finished until God's redemptive way is complete.

OTHERS UNDERSTAND THE CROSS AS AN INSTRUMENT OF RECONCILIATION

For some, the cross is repulsive, but for others it is a redemptive sign of life and hope and light. When the cross is lifted high, people come to recognize it as an instrument of reconciliation.

The word *reconciliation* is not difficult to understand. To reconcile is to bring together what has been separated; to reclaim that which might have been lost; to restore to wholeness what has been broken.

Paul wrote to the Corinthians, "In Christ God was reconciling the world to himself, not counting their trespasses against them, and entrusting the message of reconciliation to us" (II Corinthians 5:19). It was necessary for the "Word to become flesh" in order for God to "reconcile the world to himself." When we lift high the cross, we are reminded that the broken experiences of life may yet serve a purpose in God's providence. If so, then our response should be to serve as agents of that reconciling power in human lives and human events.

The late Jameson Jones, former president of Iliff Theological Seminary, gave a legendary account of a day when there was a great crowd of people gathered before the judgment of God. As God began to pronounce judgments, a cry of protest went up from the people. "Unfair! What right did God have to pass judgment upon people's lives on earth? What could God know of the agony of human pain and fear and temptation? What knowledge did God have of the suffering that could result from change and circumstance or the accident of birth? God is removed from our struggles." From the midst of the crowd a voice cried, "If God would judge us, let God be born on earth and see what it is like!" Soon there were many voices shouting: "Yeah, let God be born to poverty to live among the have-nots. Let God belong to a minority race and see what prejudice is like! God needs to know the heartbreak in a friend's betrayal or a broken trust. Let God see what it is like to be at the mercy of those who act on hearsay and rumor. Let God look into the eyes of arrogant hatred and suffer the violence of a mob! Yeah, God needs to know about human life before judging us."

All of a sudden the screams began to give way to a strange silence. For somewhere, someone had called out the name of Jesus Christ. One by one they began to realize that this is what he had been. Jesus had been born to this earth, of a minority race. He had known poverty and the sweat of hard work. Jesus had suffered betrayal and knew what it was to be in the hands of those who despised him. He had looked into the eyes of hatred and heard the voice of the mob and the roar of a riot. He had suffered the agony of the cross, had known what it was to die. God in Christ had known human life to its depths.

To lift high the cross means that we recognize not only that "God was in Christ . . . reconciling the world to himself," but also that God has "entrusted the ministry of reconciliation to us." The ministry of reconciliation is something we do.

A pastor was invited to speak to a women's missionary unit on the mission of their church. She was told to be present at ten o'clock in the morning for her presentation. When she arrived, the women were involved in a planning meeting for the spring bazaar. For more than thirty minutes she listened to them aggressively debate who would bring what to sell at the bazaar. Who would bring the pickled peaches or the orange marmalade? Who would bring the apple butter or pear preserves?

After considerable discussion, the president finally turned to the pastor and said, "We are now ready to hear your program on our church's mission." At this point the pastor asked the president what had happened to her request that the missionary society sponsor a day-care ministry for the children who lived in the neighborhood surrounding their church building.

The president was visibly embarrassed and said, "I am sorry; we have not done anything on the project. I have tried, without success, for nearly five months to get someone to chair our committee on Christian Action." The pastor's response, under her breath, as she moved to the podium was, "Isn't it true—'pickled peaches and apple butter are easier made than Christians.'"

We in the church have discovered that it is easier to get involved in things like constructing buildings, repairing buildings, carpeting aisles, and cushioning pews than it is to reconcile the world to Christ. Not that these activities are evil, but we must never let them become a substitute for being an agent of God's reconciling love in a broken world.

As God's agents of reconciliation, we can let God's love be seen through us in our little corner of the world. If it is in the cross that we realize our worth as persons, then our response to others will be to help them realize their place and worth as persons. The cross should remind us that in some way we must be sure that we live our lives in such a way that this world, and the persons in it, will be better because we lived this day.

I once heard the story of a beautiful young woman who underwent surgery to remove a facial tumor. As the surgeons proceeded with the delicate operation, they inadvertently clipped a nerve that controlled the facial muscles on one side of her face. This caused a disfiguring of her face. The corner of her mouth was dramatically drawn out of shape. At first the surgeons believed that they could correct the problem with more surgery, but after the second surgery and more physical therapy, the doctors concluded that the facial condition was permanent.

The young woman's husband was present when the doctors told her that the condition could not be corrected. She turned to the wall and sobbed. At that moment the surgeon said he witnessed the most beautiful thing that he had ever witnessed.

The husband moved to the side of her bed, pulled back the sheet covering her mouth, and said, "I know you are disappointed and hurt, but you know I think your face is beautiful." He bent down, twisted and shaped his own lips to fit her mouth, and kissed her. Then he said, "See—the kiss still works."

The cross reminds us that God was in Christ, reshaping the kiss, reconciling the world to himself. God has now entrusted us with this ministry to the world. Each time we lift high the cross we are told to remember that although the cross may be repulsive, foolishness and folly to some, for us it is a constant reminder of God's redemptive and reconciling love and Christ's call to us to be agents of his redemptive and reconciling spirit in the world.

2

When You Lose Your Way, Lift High the Cross

John 10:10 -
Luke 15:1- 15, 15-30

**Read
John 14:5-6.**

Monte Sano is a mountain that overlooks the city of Huntsville, Alabama. At the peak of Monte Sano, there is a lighted cross that is visible to the city below.

Some years ago an article appeared in the *Huntsville Times* a few days before Easter, telling of a little girl who was lost in one of the large shopping malls. When the security officers questioned her about where she lived, the little girl answered, "I do not know my address, but if you will take me to the cross I can find my way home."

last

There is an old gospel hymn called "The Way of the Cross Leads Home." The text of the hymn is this:

> I must needs go home by the way of the cross *X*
>   There's no other way but this.
> I shall ne'er get sight of the Gates of Light
>   If the way of the cross I miss.

The way of the cross leads home,
The way of the cross leads home,
   It is sweet to know, as I onward go,
The way of the cross leads home.

Are the words of the old hymn true? Does the "way of the cross" lead to God? There are those who contend that is one way but imply there are other ways.

Charles Schultz, the "Peanuts" cartoonist, used to contribute youth cartoons for a former Christian family magazine, *Together*. The cartoon normally appeared on the youth page. The image of one of these cartoons has remained with me over the years. The scene is a church youth meeting. Standing in front of the group is a teenage character wearing a primitive, multicolored, witch doctor's ritual mask. The captions beneath the cartoon read: "My program tonight is entitled, 'It matters not what you believe, only whether you are sincere or not.'"

The question is, "Will any path, sincerely pursued, eventually lead a person to God?"

For a Christian, the cross of Jesus Christ is at the center of what we believe about God. God was, is, and ever shall be as revealed in the Christ of the cross. God has entered into our common humanity to do for us what we could not do for ourselves. The cross of Christ has made the *way* to God open for everyone. The only barrier to God's love and mercy is within ourselves.

Consider for a moment a few of the many ways by which people have sincerely sought God.

The pyramids in the Egyptian desert reveal the way some, as far back as 5,000 years, pursued God. In one of the pyramids along the Nile river is the body of

Cheops, Child of the Sun, Ruler of the Universe, and
Pharaoh of Egypt. His was a different pathway to God.
He believed that every day the sun was swallowed by the
goddess of darkness to pass through her body at night
and be born again with the sunrise. He believed that at
death he, too, would be swallowed by this goddess, and
that he would be born again with the sun, to ride at the
side of his father beyond the gates of the stars. In the
sands beside the great pyramid, you may see the solar
boat, thirty-feet long, fashioned from the cedars of
Lebanon to carry Cheops and all his court in an eternal
orbit across the heavens. This was his religion. He
believed in it, lived by it, and died by it.

Four thousand years ago, when Abraham journeyed
from Ur of Chaldees into the land of the Canaanites,
he found another very religious people. Their upward
path was by the way of Astarte, goddess of love and
fertility. The ruins of the magnificent columned temple
at Baalbek, in Syria, reminds us of the religious life of
these ancient people. In the temple thousands of priest-
esses served as holy prostitutes in indescribable orgies
of immoral debauchery and paganistic worship. This
was their religion. They believed in it, lived by it, and
died by it.

Two thousand years ago, pious Jewish pilgrims by the
thousands made their way to Jerusalem into the temple
on Mount Moriah. There the high altar was a rock,
believed to be the very rock on which Abraham offered
his son, Isaac. The rock was coursed and worn by the
flow of gallons of blood drawn from the veins of sacrificial goats and bullocks as an atonement for sin. This
was their religion. They were sincere. They believed in
it, lived by it, and died by it.

At the break of dawn in a humid hotel room in Amman, Jordan, I was awakened by a mournful cry outside my window. In the middle of the street was an Arab man, kneeling on a rug. With water from a battered aluminum teakettle, he carefully washed his hands, feet, and face in a ritual of purification. He then prostrated himself toward Mecca and began the first of five prayers that he, and millions of other devout Muslims, would pray that day. This is his religion. He is sincere. He believes it, lives by it, and is willing to die by it.

Inside the church of the Holy Sepulchre in Jerusalem is the marble slab believed by many to be the very table on which the crucified body of our Lord was laid out for anointment and prepared for burial. Kneeling beside that slab is a little pilgrim. She has come from afar to this most blessed and sacred place. She makes the sign of the cross. She kisses the slab again and again. She carefully rubs each prayer bead against the sacred stone. Then, with outstretched hands, she scoops up an unseen substance from the slab and rubs and bathes her body with the magical blessedness. Finally, completely covered by the protective and healing blessedness, she arises to go. On her face is the rapture of piety and ecstasy. This is her religion and she is sincere. She believes in it, lives by it, and is willing to die by it.

Picture in your mind an African woman, deep in the African bush. She wrings the head of a chicken and lets the blood squirt down onto a mud idol. It is her way of offering thanks for the healing of a sick child. This is her religion and she is sincere. She believes in it, lives by it, and is willing to die by it.

In this brief panoramic view of historical and contemporary religion, we discover three truths.

HUMAN BEINGS INSTINCTIVELY SEEK A WAY TO GOD

Seeking after God is not the result of outward circumstance nor is it stimulated by fear of crises. It is motivated from within, a gnawing hunger for God and longing for the peace of communion with one's Creator. Like the instinct that draws a migratory bird to the northern nesting ground, so there is ingrained in the very fiber of the human soul this instinct calling us to God.

As Christians, we know why this instinct for God is implanted in us. We know that we were made by God, in the image of God, for communion with God. Greater than any other impulse is our instinctive longing for God. We must find something to give ourselves to that is greater than and beyond ourselves as we seek to satisfy the frustrations of our finiteness, our weakness, our guilt, and our lostness. We have an instinct for God that must be satisfied. This is why some seek God in physical form as an idol, or in one's business, or in a cause, or in some organized system of religion. The expression of this unique and universal instinct for God is what we call "religion."

RELIGION IS, MORE OFTEN THAN NOT, EXPRESSED BY PERSONS REACHING UP FOR GOD

Consider the upward thrust of the monoliths of Egypt, the upward reach of the broken pillars of the temple of Jupiter in Athens, the towering alabaster minaret of a mosque in Cairo calling faithful followers to prayer, or the steeple of a country church on a grassy hillside—pointing like a finger to God. Religion is humankind instinctively reaching, seeking God.

We have been told that what this world now needs is religion. Politicians and philosophers, teachers and preachers have been calling for a "return to religion." However, we have never been without religion. We could no more live without religion than we could live without air to breathe. As Paul found in Athens, we find that people turn to a thousand different gods every day. The primitive worships a god of mud, while the brilliant university professor worships a god of science. A Hindu mother in India pours out her sacrifice before a god of bronze, while countless numbers of people make a god of wealth and health, status and fame. Religion is everywhere. Religion is the upreach of persons for God.

WE DO NOT GET TO GOD BY THE WAY OF RELIGION

All the religion in the world cannot reconcile us to God. Christianity is not a religion. Christianity and religion are opposites.

Christianity and religion are opposites in *direction.* Religion is the upward reach of persons to God; Christianity is the downward reach of God for persons.

Christianity and religion are opposites in *motivation.* Religion is created out of our need for God; Christianity stems out of God's grace and love for us.

Christianity and religion are opposites in *initiation.* Religion is a frustrated person searching for God; Christianity is a compassionate God seeking the person.

Christianity and religion are opposites in *salvation.* Religion is predicated on the belief that we can save ourselves by acts of worship, rites, ritual, deeds, good works, service, and devotion. In Christianity we are saved, not by what we do in penitence and sacrifice, but by what God has already done by his sacrifice of Jesus Christ.

It is not turning to religion, but turning from religion to Christ that will deliver us. Our salvation lies not in what we do for God, but in how we respond to what God has already done for us on the cross. Our message is not that of the Old Testament prophets of religion calling persons to come to God. We are New Testament evangels proclaiming that God has come to us through God's incarnate son, Jesus Christ.

Use your imagination. Picture two cliffs divided by an impassable chasm of separation. The chasm is a result of erosion of centuries of sin. Cut deep and wide, this great abyss separates humanity and God. We, humanity, stand on one side. Instinctively we know that somewhere on the other side is God, the one who created us, the one to whom we belong. The obvious thing to do is to find some way to bridge the gap in order to have communion with God.

The bridges we build to God we call "religion." Some of these bridges are broad and massive, and there are many persons who labor to build them. Other bridges are small, with a single builder and only a few travelers. Some bridges reach out farther toward God than others since they are more ethical, more acceptable philosophically, or more appealing to the mystical, scientific, or spiritual mind.

On the other side of this chasm is God. With a broken heart God surveys the frantic and futile efforts of people trying to save themselves. By the grace that was in God's heart from the foundation of the world, God said, "I will build a bridge over to humanity and open up a way for salvation and restoration." And so the Bible proclaims that "in the fullness of time, God sent forth his Son." The bridge was built. Through Jesus Christ, God built a bridge to us because we could not get to God.

For thirty-three years Jesus was "Emmanuel," God with us. Again and again Jesus explained his mission from God to the world. "The Father and I are one" (John 10:30). "Just as the living Father sent me" (John 6:57)." "For God so loved the world that he gave his only Son" (John 3:16*b*). With many miracles, signs, and indisputable demonstrations of his deity, he drove down the stakes again and again to make secure this end of the bridge. He fed the thousands, healed the blind, made the lame to walk, and cured the demon possessed. Finally, he stood by the tomb of Lazarus and prayed, "Father . . . that they may believe that you sent me." And he called with a loud voice, "Come out!" (John 11:41-43). And he who had been dead four days came out alive.

When all things had been accomplished, Jesus was betrayed and arrested. He passed through a night of abuse and torture at the hands of cruel men, and finally was sentenced to die because he "claimed to be God." On that Friday, they led him out of the city to a hill called Golgotha.

They stretched his body on a cross and drove great nails through his hands and feet. The soldiers hoisted the heavy cross into the air, tilted it, and dropped it into the hole. For six hours he hung there, forsaken by his disciples, jeered by the crowd, tormented by his enemies, and railed at by the thief.

Finally, he lifted his face to God and cried, "It is finished" (John 19:30). The tormentors must have screamed in delight, "Hear him. He is delirious. He is finished. We shall never again hear of the carpenter of Nazareth."

They were wrong. He was not finished. Three days later, he came up from the grave, alive forevermore. As the living Lord, he has marched through the centuries gathering millions in his company. He was not finished; it was finished. *Bridge of reconciliation*

What was finished? The bridge! God's way of salvation. The bridge of reconciliation, built first in the heart of God from the foundation of the world and finished at Calvary. Standing by that bridge Jesus says, "I am the way, the truth, and the life; no one comes to the Father, except through me." The way to God, to reconciliation and communion with God, is through Jesus Christ.

We do not come to the living God over the bridge of any religion. We do not come to God by the bridge of religious rites and acts of worship. We do not come to God by way of the bridge of the church. We do not come to God by way of the bridge of baptism. We do not come to God over a bridge built of our good works and moral behavior. The way to God is the way of Jesus Christ. *God does it in Christ*

The good news that is ours to proclaim is that every person stands within a few steps of this bridge with the promise of Jesus that "he who comes to me, I will not cast out." The first step onto the bridge is repentance. *1st step on bridge*

repent

To repent means to turn from every other way, every other hope, every other bridge, every sin, and turn to Jesus as the way. The second step is to believe. Believe on the bridge. We may believe it is a bridge and know all the facts about when and where, and how, and by whom it was built, but this knowledge and belief about the bridge never gets us to the other side. When we believe on the bridge, exercise our will as free moral agents, and start walking in trust across that bridge, putting the safety and destiny of our lives on it—only then does the bridge bear us up to the other side. The glorious good news of the gospel is that any person can come to Jesus. By these two simple steps we can pass over from death to life and be reconciled to God.

A number of years ago, the Archbishop of Paris preached in Notre Dame Cathedral. He shared with the congregation the story of an incident in that cathedral that happened forty years before.

There were three students touring Paris. They came into the cathedral to look it over. They were cynical and rude young men who thought all religion was a fraud. Two of the students dared the third to go into the confession box and make a bogus confession to the priest.

They badgered the student until he agreed. He did just what he was dared to do; he entered the confession booth and made a bogus confession. The old priest listened to the student's confession, knowing there was no truth in it. He listened to the false confession, sensed the student's arrogance and said, "Very well, my son, every confession requires a penance, and this will be yours. I ask you, I dare you, to go into the chapel and stand before the crucifix, look into the face of the crucified Christ and say 'All this you did for me, and I don't give a damn.' Not once, but three times you are to repeat the words."

The student swaggered out of the confession box, his friends waiting on him. He boasted of completing the dare and told them about the penance the priest required he make. His friends insisted that he would have to do what the priest asked him to do if he expected to collect on the wager.

Slowly the student approached the high altar and stood before the crucifix. He looked up into the face of Christ and slowly repeated, "All this you did for me, and I don't give a damn." The second time he said it, and the third time he could hardly get the words out of his mouth. Very slowly he said, "All of this . . . you did . . . for me . . ." and in a whisper, "and I don't give a . . ." He never finished the sentence. He went back to the confession booth and asked the priest to hear his true confession.

The Archbishop told the congregation that this was the start of a painful experience that changed this student's life and finally brought him to the priesthood. Then he told them that that was over forty years ago, and that he was that young student. Has the cross won your heart; claimed your life? You know, it takes a mighty hard heart to be unmoved in the face of the cross. Little wonder that Isaac Watts could write:

When I survey the wondrous cross
on which the Prince of Glory died,
my richest gain I count but loss,
and pour contempt on all my pride.

Were the whole realm of nature mine,
that were an offering far too small;
love so amazing, so divine,
demands my soul, my life, my all.

3

When You Feel Ashamed, Lift High the Cross

Read
John 8:1-11;
Luke 22:54-62.

Aprayer of confession some-times used in worship asks this of God: "Make us ashamed of our offenses against you and against one another." Seems sort of strange to be asking God to make us ashamed or to give us guilt feelings. Isn't that unhealthy? Isn't it true that guilt feelings are bad for us? Yet we know what it means to be ashamed of things we do; we all know what it means to feel guilty, and sometimes our guilt gets us down.

After I had corrected our three-year-old grandson, Dillon, for disobeying me, I made him come in the house and sit on the couch in the family room. He was crushed and angry with me. While he sat on the couch struggling to hold the tears back, I sat in another chair looking at him. I was somewhere between being angry and feeling guilty for correcting him. When he saw me looking at him, he said, "Don't look at me, Pooh!" I still looked at him, but now the severeness in my eyes changed to compassion and understanding. He had disobeyed; he had disappointed me; more than that, he was disappointed in himself, and now was suffering pain in being comforted by one he loved.

A similar episode occurred in the life of the disciple Peter. All the disciples were in the Upper Room. Jesus suggested that before the night was over, all his disciples would abandon him. Peter, with all intentions of being a faithful disciple, replied that, even though the rest would run away, he would not. Jesus, because he knew so well how people act in great temptation, responded by saying that before the night was past, Peter would deny him three times.

You know the story. Jesus was arrested, and the disciples fled; but when Peter came to his senses, he returned to the scene of Jesus' trial. Then the test took place. He was accused of being mixed up with the prisoner. Loyalty took a backseat, and Peter denied that he even knew Jesus.

As Jesus was being moved from Caiaphas's house, he turned and looked at Peter. Oh, the shame Peter must have felt as he saw the dejected eyes of the Master come his way! How crushing it is to be caught in the act; to be reminded that we are not faithful; to have our disobedience underscored by eyes that have seen and know. We read that Peter wept bitterly; we can imagine him covering his face, sobbing, "Don't look at me!"

Peter hated to have Jesus look at him, but at the look of Jesus, Peter recognized his own sin—and how depressing that is! Nothing is more difficult to overcome than the agony of the conscience. Peter was a man who betrayed his Lord; and in so doing, he had also betrayed himself. Yet, within Jesus' look there was not bitterness and hatred. In character with his whole ministry and his attitude toward persons in general, there was within those eyes the look of understanding and forgiveness.

GOD'S LOVE SOOTHES OUR GUILT AND HEALS OUR SHAME

Christ's compassion for Peter is consistently the picture we have of Christ as he portrayed what God is like. It is just one more example of the way in which God accepts each one of us, despite the severity of our faults. It points up so beautifully the divine economy—as God's Son is sent to obtain for us the salvation that we are unable to earn for ourselves. Yet, we still try to avoid the eyes of God, who might find us out. We dread the thought of an all-knowing God and the omnipresent eyes that note the fall of a sparrow and our disobedience. "Don't look at me!" becomes the repeated refrain of guilt-ridden humanity.

We have the pictures of Adam and Eve in Genesis, hiding in the garden after their rebellious deed in the hope that they could escape the reprimanding eyes of God: "They heard the sound of the LORD God walking in the garden at the time of the evening breeze, and the man and his wife hid themselves from the presence of the LORD God among the trees of the garden. But the LORD God called to the man, and said to him, 'Where are you?'" (Genesis 3:8-9).

That is always the way it is. We want to cry out, "Don't look at me!" but God is always asking, "Where are you?" You see, the creator God cannot tolerate a relationship that is broken and deteriorating. We want to hide the loose ends, but God is continually trying to splice them.

God never ceases to find us in spite of our efforts to hide our faces. The methods God uses are strange. We think we have outgrown the guiding hand of God; then we are faced with a situation far beyond our strength or ability to handle. We think we can find fulfillment and peace of mind through material goods, but we find our desires too bottomless to fill, or we find ourselves bored or anxious. We think we have failed too completely to warrant the presence of God, but we feel his comfort. In our own defense we want to yell, "Don't look at me!" but we rejoice at God's answer: "Where are you?" Oh, the joy when we think we are lost, and God declares that we are found!

It is a fact that, while we try in every way and wish with all our heart that God will not see us in our guilt and shame, it is only the compassionate and forgiving eye of God that can soothe our guilt and heal our shame. The Bible is full of such phrases as, "He looked on them and had compassion." We are consistently reminded that the pure eyes of God always point out our weaknesses in contrast; yet the glance of those eyes is necessary for us to feel forgiven and freed of exactly what we hate being.

In the case of Adam and Eve, it was only as God looked upon the sins of floundering humanity that we received the guidance of the prophets, and ultimately the salvation of the Christ. God saw where we were, and declared to us that, through his forgiveness, we were pure and could once again tolerate his look.

In the case of Peter, it was only after Jesus had looked at Peter, bringing to a head Peter's feelings of remorse and assuring him of his love, that Peter surged to become a leader of God's church and was enabled to respond to Christ's departing words: "Peter, follow me . . . feed my lambs" (author's paraphrase).

It was Jesus on the cross who, as he looked at one and then another of his betrayers, said: "Father, forgive them; for they know not what they do." *Forgiving Eyes.*

This is the result of the look of Christ upon us. His eyes are forgiving, even though we falter and fall because we do not see the dismaying consequences of what we are doing. God understands our guilt and restores to us the joy of life.

How hopeless our lives would be if we were forever to hide our face from God's eyes, if we were not to pray that God would look upon our situation with the fullness of his love and acceptance, or if we were not anxious to look back into his eyes with a prayer of thanksgiving for having been found. If we are not conscious of the eyes of God, we may never feel the compulsion to ask forgiveness. If God does not look, we *Need for Gods eyes on us* may never know the compassion and acceptance with which he deals with us. If we do not look back into the eyes of God, we may never know the assurance that keeps on looking and caring and loving. The power of God's grace says we don't have to be ashamed. God's love enfolds us, upholds us, and overwhelms us. What a marvelous thing it is!

GOD'S LOVE FREES US FROM THE PAST

Young people who are in the midst of identity confusion—groping for new vocation and experiencing
surging emotions, oftentimes estranged from parents
and friends—need to understand that the gospel of
Jesus Christ is a freedom from shame or self-conscious-
ness that so often condemns us in our own eyes.

Those of us who know what it means to do things we
regret or are ashamed of need to know that the life lived
out of an acceptance of grace, according to the gospel,
does not require or expect a perpetual grinding of
regret. This knowledge sets us free. We cannot undo
the past, but God releases us from the past. Nowhere
in the gospel is God pictured as an arrogant God who
points an accusing finger of judgment upon his people,
but every gesture of our Lord Jesus Christ was filled with
a gracious openness to all.

Jesus consorted with those whom others said were
sinners and outcasts, the social degenerates of his day.
He was criticized for this, because he was not careful
enough or selective enough or discriminating enough
in the way he offered the grace and goodness of God.

While Jesus was teaching in the Temple, the scribes
and Pharisees brought to him a woman who had been
caught in the act of adultery. The religious leaders
asked Jesus, "What will you do with her? The law says
she should be stoned" (author's paraphrase). Jesus
bent down to write on the ground. When they continued to question him, he said, "Let anyone among you
who is without sin be the first to throw a stone at her"
(John 8:7). Gradually, they all walked away, leaving the
woman alone with Jesus. He said to her, "'Woman,

where are they? Has no one condemned you?' She said, 'No one, sir'" (vss. 10-11).

Then he said, "Neither do I condemn you; go and sin no more."

What a beautiful thing Jesus did for the woman. He did not want to add to her shame. His response to her reveals that we do not have to be ashamed but can hold our heads high—not with pride that comes from claiming our attainments, but with a kind of natural innate dignity that comes because we are God's children and because God loves us and cares for us. We can see each other in our genuine need and speak to that need and love each other and hold each other's hands like family, which we are: the household of faith.

When you feel ashamed, lift high the cross, and remember that Jesus died to rid you forever of shame and guilt.

Following the end of World War II in Germany, an American chaplain was stationed in West Berlin as a part of the occupying forces. One Sunday, following church, he was invited to lunch by a German couple.

Following lunch, when they were sitting in the parlor, the chaplain noticed a child's pair of old and worn-out shoes sitting on the mantle. The couple explained that their nine-year-old had been a war orphan. They found him one day wandering around among the bombed-out rubble. They took him home with them and soon after, they officially adopted him as their own. Then the father walked over to the mantle and took the shoes in his hands and explained that these were the shoes that young Hans was wearing when they found him. The father added, "We keep them here as a reminder to Hans of where he came from. Whenever he disobeys or misbehaves, we take the shoes down and show them to him to remind him of what we have done for him."

The American chaplain said that he could not keep from watching Hans as the boy's father told the story about the old shoes. Hans sat there downcast and ashamed. The chaplain thought to himself, "How wonderful it is to have a heavenly father who does not take out our old shoes and shame us, but forgives and forgets the past and sets us free to live today, and for the rest of our lives."

When we lift high the cross, we are reminded that we don't need to be ashamed anymore.

4

When It Is Hard to Forgive, Lift High the Cross

Read
Luke 9:23-25;
Matthew 18:21-35.

We live in a society where sin's moral decay threatens our very civilization. We know of starvation throughout the world. At the same time, the world continues to be consumed by materialism, getting and spending. Millions are homeless or live in destitute circumstances. War is rampantly killing thousands of innocent children in Bosnia, Liberia, and the Middle East. Crime and violence in the streets and in our schools bring a warlike atmosphere to our very doors. The unbridled use of drugs and alcohol is an evil in our anesthetized society that has reached alarming proportions. Racism continues to flourish. Add to this brief list the unkindness and subtle violence we inflict on one another, especially those closest to us—our families, friends, and associates.

Sin is a fact. Our need is to repent of our sin before God and to accept the free gift of God's forgiving love in Jesus Christ. "For by grace you have been saved through faith, and this is not your own doing; it is the gift of God" (Ephesians 2:8).

The cross is where we go. Because of the cross, we have the assurance of God's forgiving grace. There is nothing you can do to make forgiveness possible. In the words of the old hymn, "In my hand no price I bring . . . simply to thy cross I cling." It is not by who we are or by who we know or by what we have or by what we have done, but by God's love that we are forgiven.

Not only does the cross of Christ make grace possible to us and assure us of our forgiveness, but the cross also challenges us to extend the same grace and forgiveness to others. Jesus makes it clear that the life of forgiveness is the Christian disciple's way of life. "And to all he said, 'If anyone wishes to be a follower of mine, he must leave self behind; day after day he must take up his cross, and come with me'" (Luke 9:23 NEB).

The only way to understand what Jesus meant is to contend with his perception of his own cross and then, in the light of that, the cross of those who would choose to follow him. Jesus knew who he was and why he had come into the world. He was the lamb of God come to take away the sins of the world. When the disciples began to understand that he was the Son of God, he began to teach them about his death on the cross. His teaching was clear: he would be the suffering servant, the sacrifice for the sins of the world. Atonement and forgiveness would be the purpose of his death.

Jesus called persons who would follow him to take up their crosses daily. Did he mean they were to go to Jerusalem to share his fate? Did he mean that they would all suffer a martyr's death? Or was there something more significant in the call to take up a cross and follow him? One thing is for sure, not until we discover and experience the essential purpose and power of Christ's cross will we be able to accept and appropriate the demand of the cross given to us.

WHEN IT IS HARD TO FORGIVE, WE NEED TO REMEMBER WHAT JESUS TAUGHT ABOUT FORGIVENESS

Forgiveness and reconciliation were at the heart of Jesus' understanding of his death on the cross. The crosses that we are to assume are extensions for all time of that same forgiving love. Christians are to be forgiving persons. As God sent Jesus into the world to reveal God's forgiving nature, so too, we are sent to imitate that same forgiving spirit in all our relationships.

Over and over Jesus sought to drive this point home with his disciples. He said, "This is how you should pray. . . . Forgive us the wrong we have done, as we have forgiven those who have wronged us" (Matthew 6:9-12 NEB).

Peter asked Jesus, "'Lord, how often am I to forgive my brother if he goes on wronging me? As many as seven times?' Jesus replied, 'I do not say seven times; I say seventy times seven'" (Matthew 18:21-22 NEB).

Jesus followed this response with a parable. Jesus told of a king who decided to settle accounts with his servants. There was a servant who owed him a fortune. Since the servant had no means of repaying him, the

[handwritten margin notes: "servant who was forgiven but did not forgive his fellow servant"]

king ordered him, along with his wife and children, to be sold to meet the debt. The servant fell at his feet and cried for mercy. He promised that if given time he would repay the debt in full. The king was touched by the plea of the servant and canceled his debt completely.

[handwritten margin note: "did not forgive"]

The servant, with his debt canceled, went out to celebrate. He encountered a fellow servant who owed him a small debt. The servant grabbed the fellow servant by the throat and told him to pay him what he owed him. The fellow servant fell to his knees and asked mercy and promised to pay in time. The man refused and had him jailed until he could pay his debt.

[handwritten margin note: "would not forgive"]

Others were distressed and they went to the king and told the whole story. He accordingly sent for the man. "You scoundrel!" he said to him; "I remitted the whole of your debt when you appealed to me; were you not bound to show your fellow-servant the same pity. . . ?"

[handwritten margin note: "Matt"]

(18:32-33 NEB). The king was so angry that he condemned the man to punishment until the servant was able to pay the debt in full.

[handwritten margin note: "looks us, we must forgive"]

Jesus concluded the parable by saying, "And that is how my heavenly Father will deal with you, unless you each forgive your brother from your hearts" (vs. 35).

[handwritten margin note: "forgive"]

Jesus continually warned that we cannot be forgiven if we do not forgive. "And when you stand praying, if you have a grievance against anyone, forgive him, so that your Father in heaven may forgive you the wrongs you have done" (Mark 11:25 NEB).

One of the first Bible verses that I can recall memorizing was, "Be ye kind one to another, tenderhearted, forgiving one another, even as God for Christ's sake hath forgiven you" (Ephesians 4:32 KJV). As a child I loved that verse, and I thought, of course, we'd soon all act that way. The truth is, forgiving is not all that easy or that widely practiced. Many of those who claim to be disciples find it difficult to forgive. How sad! This is what it means to be a Christian: one who hears about God's love, experiences forgiveness; and then learns to extend the same forgiveness to those who need it most.

WHEN IT IS HARD TO FORGIVE, WE NEED TO REMEMBER WHAT IT MEANS TO BE FORGIVEN OURSELVES

How can we ever forgive others unless we know the joy of being forgiven? The courage for being forgiving persons comes from renewed experiences of being forgiven ourselves. Yesterday's forgiveness is not enough for today's sins and failures. When we have tasted of the freshness of God's grace for our failures, we will have fresh grace for others. Jesus said it clearly, "But the one to whom little is forgiven, loves little" (Luke 7:47).

When we become critical and judgmental, withholding forgiveness, it is a sure sign of our need of grace. We all need to realize that our inability to forgive others is related to our inability to forgive ourselves. When days drift by without our repentance, we put down our cross and for a time miss our calling to be reconcilers. Then comes the Lord's whisper in our soul: "Will you not forgive as I have forgiven you?" Do you ever have times like that?

Lifting high the cross and denying ourselves means the total reorientation of life with self no longer at the center. We give up our rights to run our own lives. Taking up our cross always spells crucifixion of ourselves. Our Calvary is to die to self-control. This includes letting go of unforgiving judgments of ourselves as well as others.

Jesus continually warned that we cannot be forgiven if we do not forgive. "Whenever you stand praying, forgive, if you have anything against anyone; so that your Father in heaven may also forgive you your trespasses" (Mark 11:25).

As a model of how we might learn to forgive, consider what happened to Pope John Paul II at St. Peter's Square in May 1981. John Paul was a man dedicated to following Jesus Christ, a man of peace, a spiritual leader of millions, a good man; and then came a gunshot, a mindless tragedy, and a fleeing gunman.

Look again. It's January 1984, Rome's Rebibbia Prison. There sits the would-be assassin, Mehmet Ali Agca, now a convicted felon. Sitting close and facing him is the Pope, gently holding the hand that held the gun and speaking words of forgiveness. Following their twenty-one minute conversation, John Paul told the press, "What we talked about will have to remain a secret between him and me. I spoke to him as a brother whom I have forgiven, and who has my complete trust."

Agca, by the way, appeared to listen very intently to the Pontiff and at the conclusion of their discussion, he bent his head over the Pope's hand, either kissing John Paul's ring or pressing the Pope's hand to his forehead in a Muslim gesture of respect. We can only guess what the Pope's visit meant to Ali Agca, but what interests many is what that visit meant to John Paul. Despite the fact that the Pontiff is unquestionably a man of God, he is also a *man*. As such, he is subject to the same temptations to bitterness and hatred that all of us experience.

Obviously, John Paul chose not to yield to any such temptation and released whatever anger and other poison that had accumulated as a result of the attack by forgiving Ali Agca, just as Jesus would have done. Can we too find that same freedom from self-destructive bitterness after we have been wounded in the arena of life?

WHEN IT IS HARD TO FORGIVE, WE NEED TO REMEMBER THAT GOD GIVES US THE GRACE TO BE FORGIVING PERSONS

Just think what God demands of us, God enables us to do by giving us the grace we need to do it. St. Augustine said, "Demand what thou wilt, but first, give me what Thou dost demand!" That is exactly what God does, and we call that loving initiative *grace*. Nowhere is that grace more miraculously demonstrated than in Christ's death on the cross.

I moved to Mississippi in 1984 to assume my responsibilities as resident bishop of The United Methodist Church in Mississippi. Soon after moving I made arrangements to visit the Longdale community, located on the outskirts of Philadelphia, Mississippi. This is the location of the Mt. Zion United Methodist Church. The church was burned by members of the Ku Klux Klan on the evening of June 16, 1964. The church had been voter-registration headquarters and freedom school during the civil rights movement in Neshoba County.

Bud and Beatrice Cole are active leaders in the Mt. Zion Church. They, along with nine other church officers, had been attending a stewards' meeting at the church on the night of June 16, 1964. As they were leaving the meeting they were assaulted by a large group of white men. Some of them wore Klan robes and hoods. The Coles were attacked as they got into their car to drive home. Bud was dragged from the automobile and brutally beaten. He was cursed, kicked, and stomped by these men. Beatrice was forced to watch. When Bud was down on the ground, they continued to kick him until he was unconscious. Beatrice said, "One of the men said 'we'll keep on beating him until he wakes up.'"

They stopped beating Bud, and Beatrice went to him, cradling his broken head in her lap as the attackers drifted back to their cars and pickups. They gunned their engines and slowly pulled out of the churchyard. She helped Bud to his feet, and they staggered to their car.

Somehow Bud managed to drive them home. He refused to let Beatrice go for a doctor until morning. He thought the white men might be lurking about. He lay in his bed moaning the rest of the night, while Beatrice sat up with him attempting to tend to his wounds.

A little before 1:00 A.M., the Coles and the other residents of the area heard a single car speed up the Longdale road toward the church, and a few minutes later they heard the same vehicle roar back from the same direction. Not long after, Beatrice observed an eerie glow in the sky. The church was on fire.

The next day, after confirming that the church had been destroyed, Beatrice took Bud to Philadelphia, the county seat of Neshoba County, where the dentist set his broken jaw. The doctor set his broken leg and taped his broken ribs.

A few days later, three young friends of the Coles came to visit. They were interested in the Coles and the Mt. Zion Church burning. Beatrice served them some ice-cold Kool Aid. They talked. The young men were civil rights workers. The Coles were the last to see them alive.

On August 4, the bodies of the young civil rights workers were removed from an earthen dam. After their visit with the Coles, while on their way back to Meridian, the young men were murdered, and buried in the earthen dam. It was a story that shocked the world.

On my first visit to Mt. Zion, I preached to an alive congregation. Bud and Beatrice were on the front row. Bud has walked with a cane ever since the beating. There are obvious scars on his face that resulted from the attack. However, there were smiles on their faces as we sang and worshiped together. After worship, I had the privilege of visiting in the Cole home. We talked at length about the events surrounding the beating and the burning of the church. They laughed and said, "Oh, that was the first burning. The Klan burned our church three more times."

There was obviously no bitterness or anger in the hearts of Bud and Beatrice Cole. Beatrice said, "We had a hard time forgiving in the beginning. We had hard feelings." Then Bud said "We've got to forgive those men. . . . If we don't forgive them, then God won't forgive us." She continued, "It still was hard. But, you know a strange thing happened. We prayed that God would forgive us for not being forgiving. And do you know what? God did! And not only that, but God gave us the strength to forgive those who hurt us. Not only the strength to forgive but to forget."

Sitting in their little living room hearing their story was an experience that I will not soon forget. I felt that I was in the presence of two of God's special children. Their story was a wonderful story of grace. It was God's marvelous gift of grace that enabled them to forgive. It is in being forgiven that we are enabled to forgive.

Christ never meant for us to lift the cross alone. God is not standing over us making demands but is at our side, helping us to do what we cannot do in our own strength. God does not merely ask us to forgive and forget, but God's grace enables us to forgive and forget.

Paul challenged the Colossians to nail their sins to a cross. The same should be true of our memories. In ancient Greece, a nail driven through a list of charges against a person and displayed publicly, meant exoneration. Paul maximizes the imagery by calling Christians to do the same. Nail it to a cross! When we do, the same love exposed on Calvary floods our memories, canceling the remembrance of our sins and those of others we have retained too long.

When it is hard to forgive, lift high the cross and remember what Jesus taught about forgiveness. Remember your own forgiveness. And never forget that God gives us the grace to be forgiving persons. When we allow the forgiving love of Christ's cross to grip our lives, we learn the secret and joy of victorious living. We are able to lift high the cross and follow him.

5

When It Is Hard to Know and Do God's Will, Lift High the Cross

Read Matthew 18:10-14; 21:28-32.

There is no question more often asked of me than this: "How can I know and do the will of God?" Many people have a wide assortment of ideas about God's will. There are many interpretations, and many of them are innocently distorted.

These distortions occur amid tragic circumstances more often than not. Often people use the phrase: "Oh well, it's the will of God," when they do not understand the event that has happened. Life's events are seen by some as circumstances that we must accept without question or complaint. Did you slip on the ice and break your arm? It was the will of God. Did your wife die of cancer? It was the will of God. Was your child killed by a drunken driver? It was the will of God. Do some nations live in luxury while others struggle to survive? It is the will of God. Will our world experience nuclear war? If it does, it will be the will of God.

How unknowingly these comments are made. How carelessly we use the phrase "the will of God." It is so important that we understand more about the will of God. I cannot help believing that there are people who have been "turned off" from Christianity by Christians attributing every occurrence in life to God, everything from a spilled bowl of breakfast cereal to the Holocaust. Worshiping a God who causes cancer, the death of children, senseless killing, and starvation is not very appealing. However, that is exactly the God that some people seem to worship.

An experience that I will always remember took place soon after I began serving my first congregation. Early one morning, one of my church members called and told me that her sister and her sister's fifteen-year-old daughter had been killed by her sister's drunken husband and that he had committed suicide. She asked if I would come. When I arrived at the home, neighbors, family, and friends were already arriving. As each greeted the family, they did so with such remarks as, "It was just God's will that this has happened." "When it is time for a person to die you can't do a thing about it. It was their time . . . that's all." Then I witnessed the family begin to repeat those same expressions as though they agreed, whether they believed it or not.

Although I truly sympathize with such persons in deep grief, such statements are the result of confused ideas about God. It would have been more truthful to say: "Drinking is the cause of so much suffering." I did not say this to the family because the time to gain a correct understanding of God and God's will is not after a crisis, but before tragedy strikes.

Was it God's will? It either was or it wasn't. We have to think of not only the end result, but also of the accumulated responsibility leading up to the incident itself. The drunken husband is either to be commended or condemned. He either did the will of God, or he did the furthest thing from the will of God.

A number of years ago a fire swept through an old, inadequate building of a Catholic parochial school in a midwestern city, trapping and bringing death to scores of boys and girls. Several days later, at a funeral mass for the victims, a Catholic priest told the grief-stricken loved ones that the fire was the will of God.

School officials and city fire inspectors had closed their eyes and risked the lives of hundreds of children by sending them to school in a building that should have been condemned. Perhaps the nuns and the priests had prayed that God would make an exception, that the saints would protect them. When the building burned to the ground, it was conceded that this must be the will of God: a building that should have been condemned; safety rules and fire drills that had been largely ignored; an accumulation of wastepaper in the basement that should have been disposed of; a delinquent student who slipped a smoke in the basement corner; a blazing inferno; a funeral; and a priest who sought to comfort his people by saying that all of this was the will of God.

Again, it either was God's will or it wasn't God's will. If it was God's will, then perhaps it is wrong for us to build fireproof buildings. Perhaps we are trying to outsmart and hinder God in doing God's will when we drill our children in the rules of safety. Shall we block God's purposes—this God who murders little children?

What can we say about God's will?

God Wills Only Good

God does not want bad things for us'

God wills only good because God is good. What we know about God's will is based on what we know about God. Our best illustration for what God is like is found in the life of Jesus. When we study the life of Jesus as recorded in the Gospels, we discover that Jesus never wished ill or hardship on any individual. Just the opposite. Every act was an act of love and compassion.

none of us ?

In Matthew 18:14, Jesus says, "It is not the will of your Father in heaven that one of these little ones should be lost." He was one who cared about those who were troubled or in trouble. He cured those who were ill. He did not cause the illness. If this is a picture of what Jesus was like, then say to yourself: "God is like that. Did Jesus love all kinds of people? So does God. Did Jesus give himself for them? So does God. Was Jesus kind? So is God. Was he good? So is God." If God was in Christ, then there is no way we can say that God wills death, destruction, war, illness, and heartache. It is simply against God's nature.

There Is a Difference Between God's Will and God's Willingness

If God's will is always good, then there must be a difference between what God wills and what God allows.

There is a philosophy of religion, or a theology of the will of God, which says that everything that happens is God's will. According to this philosophy, everything is foreordained or preordained. Everything is already decided, and we live according to fate. Nothing happens until the right number comes up and then there's no avoiding it, for "what is to be, will be." Therefore, everything that happens is God's will, according to this view.

Carl Hurley, a Kentucky humorist, tells about two brothers, Arvell and Luvell, who lived on the Rockcastle River in the mountains of East Kentucky. Their reputation for humor and antics was well-known. They were very religious. Their church taught them to believe in predestination. They sincerely believed that "what is to be, will be."

One day Arvell's mule ran away. The mule was running so fast down the side of the mountain that when he came to a bend in the road he couldn't make the turn. Instead, Arvell's mule ran headlong into a tree, which stood in the bend, and killed itself.

When Arvell was telling some of his friends about the death of his mule, someone, knowing his belief in predestination, asked him, "Was it God's will for your mule to run into that particular tree at that particular moment?" Arvell scratched his head and thought for a minute. "Well, I giss it wuz," he said, "but come to think of it, he shore had to run like the devil to make it, didn't he?"

Arvell was being inconsistent with his theology when he said that his mule "had to run like the devil" in order to do the will of God. For, according to the theology of predestination, one can do nothing to contribute to or to take away from the will of God. It is all predetermined. This kind of thinking makes humans helpless puppets, subject to the cruel sport of God who pulls strings and determines everything that happens.

There must be a difference between what God wills and what God will allow. God's will for us is good; always excellent and powerful. Anything that causes grief or separation is not what God wills, for that is what hell is: separation from God and others. Rather, "it is not the will of your Father in heaven that one of these little ones should be lost" (Matthew 18:14).

If God's will is good, then why do we experience times of grief and sorrow and suffering? The reason is that not everything that happens to us is the will of God. Far from it! If someone is killed by a drunken driver, one is wrong to say that it is the will of God. If someone is killed in a war, one is wrong to say that it is the will of God. It may be the will of the enemy, but that is a different matter. It is not the will of God.

Now, the opposite of this is to believe that God does have purpose for the world, for history, and for every individual in the world, and within this purpose God has made us free. In this arrangement there is a vast difference between God's will and God's willingness. It is this difference that we many times confuse. It is only normal. Our confusion grows out of a belief that God is all-powerful and that God would not permit awful things to happen unless he wanted them to happen. God has the power to avert tragedy; therefore, if God permits it to happen, God wants it to happen. But this is to confuse God's will and God's willingness. God has made a certain kind of world. God does not will that devastating earthquakes happen, killing families and causing homelessness and deprivation. God does not will for a man to get drunk and kill his wife and child. But God has to be willing for that to be a possible result, or we are not free.

If God's will is good and carries with it a willingness, a freedom which makes us responsible participants in it, then our primary purpose in life should be to know and do the will of God.

GOD'S WILL SHOULD BE DONE

Our trouble is not in knowing God's will as much as it is doing God's will. We already know more than we are willing to do. How can anyone seek to know more of the will of God when we have failed to respond to the revelations of God's plans that have already been made known to us?

This was Jesus' point with the religious leaders of Israel. They continued to ask questions about his authority. Jesus plainly told them that his authority came from God. Jesus had repeatedly told them this. They knew more than they were willing to act on. Their questions exposed their disobedience.

In the face of their disobedience, Jesus shared a parable, the parable of the two sons.

"A man had two sons; he went to the first and said, 'Son, go and work in the vineyard today.' He answered, 'I will not'; but later he changed his mind and went. The father went to the second and said the same; and he answered, 'I go, sir'; but he did not go. Which of the two did the will of his father?" They said, "The first." Jesus said to them, "Truly I tell you, the tax collectors and the prostitutes are going into the kingdom of God ahead of you. For John came to you in the way of righteousness and you did not believe him, but the tax collectors and the prostitutes believed him; and even after you saw it, you did not change your minds and believe him." (Matthew 21:28-32)

There was a time when one made a promise or gave one's word and you could count on it. A person's "word" was good enough to enter any agreement. Simply saying "I give you my word" was all that was necessary.

Fred Craddock, distinguished professor of homiletics at Emory University's Candler School of Theology, once told about a little boy who finally reached the age of eight.

Finally 8 years old! He is now able to play little league ball. He has a cap, much too large for his head. If it weren't for his ears, he would smother. He has a glove; he stands in front of the mirror, popping his fist into the glove and he waits and he waits and he waits that eternity before ball practice begins. He worries his mother to death. "When are we going to practice?" "I think you are to practice Tuesday, Jimmy, Tuesday afternoon." "I'd better call the coach." "Coach, this is Jimmy. When are we going to practice?" "We will practice Tuesday afternoon at 5:00, Jimmy." "Thank you, coach." The next morning, "I think I'd better check with the coach to be sure about the time for practice." He calls the coach. "We will practice at 5:00, Jimmy." "Thank you, coach." That afternoon, "I'd better check with the coach about time for practice." He calls again, "Tuesday afternoon at 5:00, Jimmy." He's worrying everyone into the ground. A little after noon on Tuesday it begins to sprinkle. The mother is ironing.

She says to Jimmy, "I sure hope it doesn't rain much. You have been anxious to begin practicing ball."

About 3:30 it really begins to rain. By 4:30 it is raining a downpour. She looks over to Jimmy: "Jimmy, I really am sorry that it is raining so hard. Jimmy, Jimmy? Jimmy?" He is already out the door, his cap on his head, his glove on the handlebars of his bicycle. Off in the rain he goes. The practice field is on the school ground. The coach, who lives across the street, looks out the windows; it's raining too hard to practice. But as he watches the rain, he sees a small boy standing where home plate once was. The small boy is up to his knees in water. The coach says to his wife, "Some stupid kid is over there on the ball field. I guess I'd better go rescue him." He puts on his rubbers and raincoat, grabs his umbrella, and swims over there. "Jimmy, what are you doing here? Can't you see it is too wet? We can't practice in this weather." Jimmy looks up at his coach and says, "I told you I'd be here, coach."

Poor Jimmy! He hasn't learned what you and I know, but we will, of course, instruct him. Don't ever say with certainty you are going to do something. You say, "If it doesn't rain, if I have the time, if things work out, if I get through my tough schedule, then I will try to be there." He'll learn, won't he?

The simple response of a little boy to his coach, "I told you I would be here," is the raw material for changing every life, every home; in fact, it is the raw material for changing the world. It is there in that simple line, "I give you my word."

On the night before Jesus was crucified, he revealed to us what he had taught in the parable of the two sons. In Gethsemane he prayed not to know the will of God, but for the strength and power to do the will of God. The mandate of the cross was revealed long before that anguished night of prayer. Because of what Jesus was faithful to do on our behalf, we can face our difficulties with confidence. God will be with us. He never leads us to do more than he will grant us strength to do.

The twist of the parable is this: Why should we have to be asked to go into the vineyard to work? Jesus was implying that if we love God, we should already be in God's vineyard at work. The *knowing* of God's will comes from constant communion with God. If we say, "I don't know what the will of God is for my life," it means that day by day we have not been listening to the leading of God's spirit that comes from prayer and communion.

When we are faithful and obedient, God uses everything we have, our minds and emotions, to impress on us what we are to do. God uses insight from others, confirmed in us by the Holy Spirit, to point the way. But the final assurance comes in personal communion with Christ. At the right moment, never too early or too late, God empowers us for doing whatever God wants done. The answer comes from the voice of God within, but more importantly, it comes while we are working in the vineyard.

GOD'S WILL WILL BE DONE

The will of God is ultimately achieved. Sometimes God achieves it through us, and sometimes in spite of us. Nevertheless, God's dreams are ultimately fulfilled.

In his book *The Will of God,* Leslie D. Weatherhead uses a good analogy to illustrate this point. He puts it this way:

> The picture in my mind is that of children playing beside a tiny stream that runs down a mountainside to join a river in the valley below. Very little children can divert the stream and get great fun from damming it up with stones and earth. But not one of them ever succeeds in preventing the water from reaching the river at last. . . . In regard to God we are very little children. Though we may divert and hinder his purposes, I don't believe we ever finally defeat them.

The water of God's purposes eventually reaches the river.

In those times in life when you do not understand what God is doing to you or is allowing to happen to you, then you need to trust where your eyes cannot see or your mind comprehend. You need to walk in the light that you do have. If you faithfully do what you see to be God's will in the circumstances that life thrusts upon you, then you can rest assured that the circumstances which God allows can never defeat the purposes which God ultimately wills. You can affirm with Paul, "For I am convinced that neither death, nor life . . . nor anything else will separate us from the love of God" (Romans 8:38-39). When this happens, you can have peace in your heart, and you shall be free to serve others with courage and joy.

6

When the Storms of Life Are Raging, Lift High the Cross

Read Mark 4:35-41.

During the summer of 1993, I was privileged to be the conference preacher for the Liberian United Methodist Annual Conference in Monrovia, Liberia. At that time the civil upheaval was at an all-time high. The warring factions had made life miserable as well as perilous for the peoples of Liberia.

It was the first annual conference that many of the pastors and lay leaders had been able to attend in several years. The theme for the conference was: "Making a Witness in the Midst of the Storm." The theme hymn was "When the Storms of Life Are Raging, Stand by Me!" The stanzas petition God "in the midst of tribulation, stand by me, when the world is tossing me

like a ship upon the sea, thou who rulest wind and
water, stand by me."

The Liberian people know what it means to live in
the "midst of the storm." During the war years the
Liberian people endured many hardships. They knew
the horrors of war firsthand—massacres, murders, loot-
ing, displacement.

On the first afternoon of the conference, the delegates saw several of their fellow pastors whom they had
not seen for three years standing in the doorway of the
conference hall. The conference broke out in sponta-
neous singing and acts of praise. They lifted the brothers to their shoulders and paraded around the hall
singing hymns. I'll never forget the sight and the sound.

At the conclusion of the week, in traditional Methodist style, the bishop stood and read the pastoral
appointments—appointments to make a witness in the
midst of the storm.

Life's storms take many different shapes. In Liberia
it may be in the form of war and displaced families. For
you, it may be that your best friend lets you down, or
sickness or death invades your family circle. It may
come in the shape of disappointment or disaster, but
no matter what shape it comes in, it constitutes a storm
for you.

There are events and circumstances and forces that
would do harm to all persons, persons of faith not
excluded. Bad things do happen to good people. The
scripture points this out. Even Jesus' disciples experience the storms. The notion is that if we're "good
enough" or "godly enough," we will not be threatened
by the storms of life. This view is widespread today, but
it simply isn't true.

Picture the scene. Evening had come and Jesus and the disciples got in the boat and sailed for the other side. Jesus was tired and went to the back of the boat and fell asleep. While he was asleep, a great storm arose, and the waves beat into the boat so that the boat filled with water. The disciples woke Jesus and said to him, "Teacher, do you not care if we perish?" He awoke and rebuked the storm. The wind ceased, and there was calm. He turned to them and said, "Why are you afraid? Have you no faith?"

Like the storms of life, the storms on the Sea of Galilee are unpredictable, frequent, and fierce. The wind comes from the eastern deserts or funnels through the mountain passes from the Mediterranean Sea. I, along with a group of friends, encountered such a storm on the Sea of Galilee. It was a frightening experience. We were traveling from Tiberias to Capernaum. When we left Tiberias, for the 45-minute boat trip, the skies were clear and the sea was calm. When we got out in the middle of the sea, everything changed. The wind began to blow, the clouds darkened, and the waves were immense. We were forced to beach the boat near Magdala. It proved to be a frightful firsthand learning experience about the sudden storms on the Sea of Galilee.

The real message of the scripture is this: there is something of the unexpected storm that invades our lives from time to time. Life is not unlike what happened to the disciples in the story. We cannot always predict how and when the storms of life will rage in our experience. Someone has said that when storms come we either act or we react. We cannot always calculate, we cannot always predict, but it's very important how we react. One thing is for sure as we live our lives day after day, storms will come. When they do, we need to lift high the cross and be reminded that it is not *from* the storm that God delivers us, but it is *in the storm*.

What is important for people of faith to remember when the storms of life are raging?

NO ONE IS EXEMPT FROM THE STORMS OF LIFE

Have you ever known any Christian who has had some tragedy befall him or her? Almost everyone has known of such a person or, in fact, has actually been that person.

The Israelites were God's people, and yet what nation, what people, could have had more trouble than they did? Their trouble and misfortune didn't mean that God had ceased caring for them and about them.

When the children of Israel were in Egypt after the death of Joseph, they began to lose the respect they had been accustomed to when one of their own had been in a position of leadership and power. Early in the book of Exodus, we are told that a king came to power in Egypt who knew nothing about Joseph and the positive contribution that Joseph and the Israelites had made to their nation.

They had thrived in a land not their own. Now the tables were turned, and the circumstances of life threatened and battered them. Contrary to the assumption that they had deserved this or that God had willed it or, worse, that bad things don't happen to good people, listen to what God said to Moses: "Then the LORD said, 'I have observed the misery of my people who are in Egypt; I have heard their cry on account of their taskmasters. Indeed, I know their sufferings, and I have come down to deliver them from the Egyptians, and to bring them up out of that land to a good and broad land'" (Exodus 3:7-8).

These were God's people, God's children, God's chosen ones; and God did rescue them. The rescue did not, however, mean a storm-free existence for the individuals and the nation. It never meant that they were free from threat. It was not to be clear sailing on calm seas. Still they were rescued, and God helped them face this and other threats.

We are God's people. As Christians who profess faith in Jesus Christ as Lord and make some effort to live by his claims, we still have our hurts and fears. We have known our share of storms, and—undoubtedly—we will experience more. The midst of the storm is a good place to remind ourselves that we are not the only persons to ever experience the storm. God has not singled us out. God sent Jesus not to explain the storm, but to fill our storms with God's grace and mercy.

FAITH IN GOD WILL HELP YOU FACE THE STORM

People are strengthened by faith in the face of the storm. I am talking not just about the great examples in the Bible and in church history, but about everyday people like you and me. You may be the kind of person who always looks to others for examples of exercising faith when it is very likely that you also are an example of someone who exercises faith courageously in dealing honestly with threat.

I am not talking about those persons who stoically ignore the storm and refuse to face it. Neither am I suggesting that the person of faith is the one who faces potentially devastating news with all smiles, without anger, without fear. I am talking about persons whose faith in God is their strength. Healing may or may not occur in their illness, but they are confident that God alone understands fully, loves to overflowing those who hurt, and never leaves them.

Annie Johnson Flint was such a person. Her grand and glorious thoughts for her poetry came in the midst of the storms of life. Her parents died when she was very young, and she had to work hard for her education. She was never free from financial worries. As a young woman she endured the encroachment of arthritis, which worsened until she was completely crippled and physically helpless. And yet she gave to the world poems of joy. The secret was in her faith in God. Her inexhaustible courage was based on the fact that God's love had no limits. God's grace cannot be measured. God's power goes beyond boundaries set by persons. That assurance was expressed in this mood-changing poem.

> God hath not promised
> Skies always blue,
> Flower-strewn pathways
> All our lives through.
> God hath not promised
> Sun without rain,
> Joy without sorrow,
> Peace without pain.
>
> But God hath promised
> Strength for the day,
> Rest for the labor,
> Light for the way,

Grace for the trials,
Help from above,
Unfailing sympathy,
Undying love.

John Claypool tells of a missionary who went out years ago to teach in a school in China. She had begun the whole venture with a deep sense of God's calling. However, in the long voyage over the Pacific by boat, all kinds of fears began to crop up. Just like Peter, who had begun in confidence but then took his eyes off Christ and let the winds drive him to terror, she too was beset by anxieties: "How will I provide for myself? Will I be able to learn the language? What will be the response of the people?" One night she went to sleep deeply troubled by all these uncertainties, and she had a vivid dream. It was as if she were standing in the middle of the Pacific Ocean all by herself with nothing but a two-by-four supporting her at the surface of the water. In that condition, a voice said to her, "Start walking to China." She answered back, "But I can't. I'm not able to walk on water. If I leave this secure standing place, I will surely drown." But the voice insisted, "I said walk. Start walking toward China." With fear and trembling, but in obedience, she lifted her foot and put it forward, and just at the moment that it was touching the surface of the water, another two-by-four, like the one on which she had been standing, appeared out of the depth. Every step she took was met by support emerging from the deep. She woke with a new sense of confidence that the scripture can be trusted: "As your days, so will your strength be."

There is something about particular crises that brings a special potency in the midst of them. And what is that "something" but the God of mercy who neither slumbers nor sleeps, with whom there is no abandonment, and who can be trusted to provide as the needs arise.

The storms of life, known and unknown, could make us so fearful that life as we know it could be squandered away in dreadful anticipation and anxiety. Faith can strengthen us. It doesn't make us blind to the storms. It doesn't ask us to close our eyes tightly enough so that all the bad things will go away. Faith does remind us of the Creator, however, and God's undying love for humanity.

GOD STANDS WITH US IN THE STORM

When we and those we love are troubled, threatened, seemingly defeated, God is still with us. There may or may not be healing; it's something to pray for. The God of wholeness certainly wants that for those who are hurting. But the assurance that God stands with us in the storms of life means victories in every episode of life. The real hope we have is that nothing in life or in death can take that from us. Paul knew it, and when he proclaimed it, he was doing more than informing. To the Romans he wrote a personal testimony to the blessedness and the ultimate power of the presence of God. "For I am convinced that neither death, nor life, nor angels, nor rulers, nor things present, nor things to come, nor powers, nor height, nor depth, nor anything else in all creation, will be able to separate us from the love of God in Christ Jesus our Lord" (Romans 8:38-39).

We do not realize the magnitude of that promise because we want more. We want the obvious resolutions, and how can we not? If the presence of God

cannot offer us more than that alone, then we wonder
What is it worth? Yet, as important as physical health
and emotional wholeness are, there is more to desire—
something much greater, the one reality that will last—
God's presence. When the waves are pounding our
lives, God's presence is what we need more than all else.
We may be out in the middle of a lake where we have
been sent and suddenly storms blow up that appear, for
all the world, about to drown us. The question arises:
where do we find the courage to keep on coping in the
midst of a life that is genuinely difficult? How do we
keep from losing control or refrain from deadening
despair? The answer is the assurance of God's presence.
This is the dimension of God's will that we can be
certain of. That is what God wants for us and what God
promises us. If we have God's presence, if God stands
with us, then we can stand the storm.

Paul, for example, could sing in prison and conquer
the worst kind of storms. The record of his personal
struggles is astonishing to review. Three times he was
beaten, once he was stoned, three times he was ship-
wrecked, a day and a night he spent in the deep. As if
that wasn't enough to test his spirit, he was also robbed,
betrayed by his friends, and ridiculed by his own people. How was he equal to the strain? Why didn't he crack
up under the pressure? The answer is simple. What
brought him through every difficulty was the faith that
his security was above the smoke and stir of this dim
spot called earth, safely in the hands of God.

Similar confidence was expressed by Martin Luther,
when he faced the Diet of Worms. He was asked,
"Where will you be, Martin Luther, when the princes of
Germany, and all your friends and family forsake you?"

"Then, as now," he calmly replied, "I will be where I have always been: in the hands of Almighty God." In reality, there was nothing to fear.

No one needs to tremble when one's life is in the hands of the power that set the stars in their courses, hung the sun and the moon in the sky, and set the earthly sphere to spinning on its axis. Awareness of that unseen reality gives a person the strength of ten. It challenges one to stand the storm and conquer the circumstance.

There is no greater need today. This is too tough a world to try to go it alone. We need all the help we can get to tackle the problems and face the storms that confused and chaotic times thrust upon us. Why be so foolish or too proud to receive the help we need by filling our human deficiencies at the wellsprings of spiritual power? If we believe there is a power in the world that is on the side of those who trust it, that sympathizes with us in our struggles, that encourages us in our despair, and that delivers us out of our trouble, the better part of wisdom is to calmly commit ourselves to its keeping.

For the challenge of weathering these stormy times without faltering and without fear, for internal strength sufficient for every trouble that living can lay upon us, for every duty that can test the spirit and tax the soul, for the critical days when work is a nightmare and every pleasure is pain, and for the hours of disappointment that take us unaware, we must build up our spiritual resources. If we substitute faith for fear as the undergirding guide for living, consciously exercise our moral muscles into sinews of strength, and trust our destiny to God, we will discover the capacity to stand the storm.

On June 8, 1993, 553 persons were massacred at the Carter Camp, a village for Firestone rubber plant employees on the outskirts of Monrovia, Liberia. The rebel leader Charles Taylor and his soldiers were, allegedly, responsible for the carnage. On the following July 11, I accompanied a group of church leaders on an inspection visit to the Carter Camp. The camp was deserted. I was asked to conduct a memorial service at nearby Harbel. The memorial service was attended by hundreds of relatives and survivors of the massacre. I was overwhelmed by the courage and faith of these people in the midst of this terrible storm.

The few remaining survivors and family members were still in the throes of grief over their dead friends and relations. But there was a peace and calm that I did not expect to see so soon after the massacre. They sang hymns. Among the hymns was "When the Storms of Life Are Raging, Stand by Me." Two of the stanzas of that hymn are an affirmation of God's faithfulness to stand with us in the storm.

> In the midst of tribulation, stand by me.
> When the host of hell assail, and my strength begins to
>   fail,
> Thou who never lost a battle, stand by me.

> In the midst of persecution, stand by me.
> When my foes in war array undertake to stop my way,
> Thou who saved Paul and Silas, stand by me.

They knew that when the storms of life were raging and the world was tossing them like a ship upon the sea, they could confidently say, "He who rulest wind and water stands by me."

7

When God Seems Silent, Lift High the Cross

Read
Psalm 22:1-2;
Job 23:1-9;
Mark 15:34.

Oh, that I knew where I might find him. . . . I would lay my case before him." This is a haunting phrase from the book of Job (23:3, 4). Imagine someone saying, "I wish I could find God." Have you ever felt that way?

Is there anybody who has not at some time or another raised the question about the very existence of God? Have you not at times asked why God was hidden or silent? Job was in that kind of mood when he uttered these words. Even if you never use the words, do you not feel that way at times?

Like Job, Elie Wiesel, who, as a child, was sent to the German concentration camps at Auschwitz and later to Buchenwald, has raised the question, "Where is God?"

In his book entitled *Night,* Wiesel tells of the awful events that occurred in the German death camps where he was a prisoner. In one episode, all the Jewish inmates were forced to line up and watch the hanging execution of three of their fellow inmates, one of them only a boy. As the victims were brought out to the gallows, someone behind Wiesel asked, "Where is God? Where is he?"

The three were executed; the two adults died quickly. Wiesel writes, "But the third rope was still moving; being so light, the child was still alive. . . . For more than half an hour he stayed there, struggling between life and death, dying in slow agony under our eyes. And we had to look him full in the face. He was still alive when I passed in front of him. His tongue was still red, his eyes not yet glazed. Behind me, I heard the same man asking: 'Where is God now?'"

That is the question of the psalmist. Where is God when you need him most? Does he no longer care? To phrase the question seems blasphemous. Who are we to question God? Even though we may hesitate to form them with our lips, the questions are still in our hearts. Oftentimes in our hurt and our anger, we want to shake our fists in the face of God and ask, "Why? Why have you abandoned me? Why have you done this to me?"

Over and over again, in the book of Psalms, we encounter the psalmist crying out to God—demanding answers, demanding action, demanding the presence of God. In fact, there are more psalms of this type, psalms of lament, than of any other category of psalms. It is to this category that Psalm 22 belongs:

My God, my God, why have you forsaken me?
Why are you so far from helping me, from the words

of my groaning?
O my God, I cry by day, but you do not answer;
and by night, but find no rest.

There is no way to know what caused the psalmist's
anguished cries to God—grief, loneliness, personal
tragedy, or depression. We don't need to know the
exact reasons because his experience is common. Life
is not fair. Life is full of pain and disappointment,
sometimes so deep that it overwhelms us.

Out of the depths of despair, the psalmist calls for
God to break his silence and make himself known. Over
and over again he pleads with God, but to no avail. "Why
art thou so far away?" He has spent sleepless nights
trying to find God, but to no avail. Where is God?

It is no insignificant thing that among the last words
Jesus uttered were words from Psalm 22. From the
depths of that lonely moment of anguish, Jesus spoke,
and the words chill our bones: "My God, my God, why
have you forsaken me?"

On the cross, Jesus experienced the lowest depths of
human suffering. Already he had experienced the loneliness of human abandonment during the long night
before the crucifixion. In the Garden of Gethsemane,
he invited his disciples to share his lonely vigil, his last
few hours of freedom there in the darkness. They
dropped off to sleep before even an hour had passed.
After his arrest, Jesus experienced the despair of human forsakenness as those who were closest to him fled
in terror, denying that they had ever known him.

Indeed these words of Jesus trouble our minds as
they break our hearts. Their expression of despair
uncovers our own despair beneath our bravado; their

echo of isolation and loneliness evokes in us our own haunting sense of aloneness. If Jesus, the incarnation of God, the Savior of the world, feels forsaken, what hope is there for us?

Through those difficult times, however, Jesus still had a strong sense of God's presence and purpose. As he died on the cross, even that sustenance seemed to leave him. Here Jesus experienced the abandonment of the one in whom he placed his trust; he felt forsaken by God. Jesus experienced the hiddenness of God, God's silence.

Samuel Beckett's *Waiting for Godot*, from the opening scene to the final curtain, wrestles with the seeming hiddenness of God. Why doesn't God say something? Why doesn't God do something to right wrong in the face of all the injustices of life? Where is God hiding? Has he gone to sleep? Doesn't he care?

It is to this extremity of despair that we need to lift high the cross. The cross speaks to the condition of God's hiddenness.

THE SILENCE OF GOD IS THE GREATEST MEASURE OF OUR BELIEVING

When we feel the farthest from God, we are perhaps closest to God. In our sense of being forsaken there is no longer any pretense. When we know we are alone, there is only raw human need, our own and that of others, that partakes of the suffering heart of God. The cross becomes our assurance that human despair can be transformed into faith. It can be the occasion for the growing of real faith.

This was true for Job. He came to realize that God was not one who could be manipulated, hoodwinked, or evaded. Through his adversities, Job came to declare a faith that would stand in defiance of anything that might happen to him.

When we cry out and God seems silent, the silence may be because God's ways are not human ways. When we pray and our prayers seem to go unanswered, it may be that God is being kind to us. Garth Brooks, the popular country and western artist, recorded a song called "Thank God for Unanswered Prayers." The song is about his thankfulness for God not granting some of his prayers. Brooks sings, "I wasn't aware at the time, but God had something better in mind."

How often we ask God for answers when our real need is to learn to ask the right questions. In the face of disappointment and suffering we cry out "Why?" The urgent issue is not some intellectual explanation of the reason for suffering, but faith to trust the resources of a heavenly father whose name is love and who will see us through any circumstance.

After preaching in a church I served more than twenty-five years ago, a man greeted me at the close of the worship service. He reminded me of who he was. I easily recalled our relationship. When I first became his pastor, he, along with his wife and two small children, were new members of the congregation. Then one day he came to me in desperation. He was in his "dark night of the soul," After ten years of marriage, his wife had left him. His world had collapsed. He was angry, hurt, resentful toward God and his wife. We met several times. After I moved from the church, I lost contact with him.

On this day, however, he was a happy man. He introduced me to his new wife whom he had met and married a couple of years after his first wife left him. He greeted me warmly, and stood around until I had finished greeting others. He thanked me for being there for him when he needed me. He shared a bit of his last twenty years. He confessed that only after much struggling was he able to make peace with God. It was several years before he returned to worship. I can still recall his anger at God. He said that the healing in his life came about after his pastor asked him to read the books of Job and the Psalms. In them he found the feelings that he had known. The reading and the counseling enabled him to deal with his feeling of anger at the hiddenness of God in his time of need.

He made a remarkable statement: "Brother Bob, God was there all the time. God never left me. I left him. But I am back!"

It is at this point that the cross speaks to all of us. Jesus' lonely words, asking why God has forsaken him, are not spoken for those who are secure in their faith. Jesus speaks for those who are lost and alone. Because Jesus on the cross experienced the worst that life had to offer, we know that God understands and is with us in all our times of suffering, loneliness, and despair. Calvary becomes our assurance that human despair can be transformed into faith.

Jesus' petition was not a cry to some abstract void; it was the desperate prayer of one who had known and lost the sense of God's presence. Even while feeling abandoned, Jesus addressed the God who seemed absent; his despair was directed to the God whom he believed. The despair was real, but underneath it God was already there. Even in the life of our Lord we see it: the seeming silence of God is not God's distance from us but our estrangement from the Creator.

The Silence of God Expresses the Mystery of God's Being

Some people are arrogant enough to think that they can figure out or apprehend God. They believe that they can manipulate God to do their bidding. It is as though they think they have God in their hip pocket.

Part of the problem with some Christians today is that they are shallow and superficial. They can be upbeat and positive with the promise that "Something good is going to happen to you today," and amid testimony of how God has materially blessed them, they proclaim a God that they want and not the God that they need. Certainly there's nothing wrong with being positive and celebrating the goodness of God. The psalms themselves often remind us of the need to praise God. But faith loses touch with reality when it allows no room for the experience of pain, loneliness, and despair that are so much a part of us.

Pascal, the French mathematician and philosopher, states that "every religion that does not affirm that God is hidden is not true. The silence of God is really the hiddenness of God . . . the mystery of his being." This mystery is almost disregarded in the popularizing of Christianity in our day. When the mystery is neglected, ignored, swept away, the divine is literally vulgarized. The God of popular religion is a kind of cross between Father Time and Santa Claus but not the God of the biblical revelation.

How glibly we moderns talk of God, when the most appropriate approach is silence. A pastor by the name of John Thompson has suggested that one of the most important verses in the Bible is Psalm 46:10, when God through the Hebrew poet states: "Be still and know that I am God." Thompson says, however, that this translation is much too tame. It does not really communicate the force of what God is saying here: "Shut up! Not with all your talking about me will you ever know me . . . not with all your speculating!" (*Pulpit Digest*, November/December 1987, p. 76).

We seem to be afraid of the silence. There is very little silence in our lives—even in worship. I recall an usher asking me to request the organist to play more softly during the prelude to worship. I was so pleased at his request for silent moments. Then he said, "The people can't hear each other talk."

There are times when nothing is more sacred than silence. There is nothing more beautiful than the silence in the house of God before the worship service begins, when one encounters the sense of awe in the presence of the holy. Silence and awe are the appropriate responses to God.

This was the experience of the Old Testament prophet Elijah when he was cowed by the blatant forces of evil personified in Jezebel. Jezebel had vowed she would kill the prophet of Jehovah, for he had humiliated her by exposing the false gods she worshiped. With this threat on his life, Elijah was literally shaking in his sandals. He sought refuge in a cave. There the word of the Lord sought him out, saying:

"What are you doing here, Elijah? . . . Go out and stand on the mountain before the LORD." . . . Now there was a great wind, so strong that it was splitting mountains and breaking rocks in pieces before the LORD, but the LORD was not in the wind; and after the wind, an earthquake; and after the earthquake a fire, but the LORD was not in the fire; and after the fire, a sound of sheer silence. (I Kings 19:9-12)

Elijah recognized the voice of God in the silence. How often we look for God in the blatant, the loud, the showy, the spectacular—the earthquake, wind, and fire; but as the prophet learned, God is in none of these. It is not the clamorous voice of humanity that has the last word, but the silence of God.

God is both hidden and present; God is both immanent and transcendent. God's revelation is so strange, so unexpected, so unbecoming to our idea of a god that we often miss the real thing.

Have you ever thought about the fact that God is both present and hidden in everything, all the time? Is this not the reason we so often miss God? God is present in every event of one's life, present in the interactions among people and nations, present in everything, yet always hidden while present. We may wonder why it is so. In part it is, no doubt, to keep us humble. There is nothing more damaging in life than the kind of pride that overreaches itself, that refuses to acknowledge its own limitations, its own self-perversity and sin. We often miss God, as people did in the first century, because the God of glory is really the God of the most commonplace.

The Silence of God Is Broken by the Magnitude of God's Final Benediction

God has the final word, the benediction. It is a blessing. The questions of God's silence and hiddenness that are present in the first two verses of Psalm 22 give way to acts of praise in the later verses. The psalmist acknowledges that God has watched over him, and then he says that all will bow down and worship God for his goodness.

The psalmist turned away from his present predicament long enough to ponder how God had acted in the past. He remembered that it was God who created the world; and it was God who had brought him forth from his mother's womb and kept him safe. By recounting the past, he found hope for the present.

Our own pasts can remind us that our God is a caring God. As we reflect on our lives and on the dealings of God throughout history with us and all God's people, comfort and confidence will be ours. In our good moments as well as in our darker moments, God is there. The God of Abraham, Isaac, and Jacob, the God of the psalmists, and the God of our own past journeys is also the God in our present pilgrimage. God is with us, even when God seems hidden or silent.

Perhaps you have never experienced the silence of God as expressed by Job and the psalmist and even our Lord hanging on the cross. Number yourself among just a few. I am convinced that there are more of us who know the hurt and loneliness of feeling separated from God. The cry of Job, "Oh, I wish that I could find God," is our cry, too. If that is your experience, then I encourage you to continue your pilgrimage of faith, learning from Job and the psalmist that moments when God seems silent and hidden can be moments of growth in your relationship with God.

There is a very beautiful story behind one of the best loved hymns. The writer of this hymn was George Matheson, for many years the pastor of one of Scotland's greatest churches. Matheson was blind and had suffered much as a result of his blindness. Among other things, his fiancée had refused to marry him, and loneliness and despair were often with him. He felt God was absent and hidden.

One afternoon, on the day of his sister's wedding, he walked back to the parish manse, and in a mood of deep reflection, sat down at his desk and wrote a hymn. Speaking of the experience later he said, "Something had happened to me that was known only to myself, and that caused me the most severe mental suffering. It was the quickest bit of work I ever did in my life. I had the impression of having it dictated to me by some inward voice rather than of working it out myself. I am quite sure that the whole work was completed in five minutes, and equally sure that it never received, at my hands, any correction or retouching."

Sitting at his desk that lonely afternoon and thinking back upon his life of blindness and pain, George Matheson said he felt the presence of God where he had felt him absent from his life for a long time. He put his pen to paper and wrote these lines:

> O Love that wilt not let me go,
> I rest my weary soul in thee;
> I give thee back the life I owe,

That in thine ocean depths its flow
    may richer, fuller be.

O Joy that seekest me through pain,
    I cannot close my heart to thee;
I trace the rainbow through the rain,
and feel the promise is not vain,
    that morn shall tearless be.

O Cross that liftest up my head,
    I dare not ask to fly from thee;
I lay in dust life's glory dead,
and from the ground there blossoms red
    life that shall endless be.

Sometimes it seems to us, even as for a moment it seemed to Jesus, that God is silent or hidden. However, if we will wait with faith and patience, as he did, in time, the "dark night of the soul" gives way to morning. For us, as it was for our Lord, the light begins to break; gradually our question marks are straightened into exclamation points. Our last words are not "My God, my God, why have you forsaken me?" (Matthew 27:46)—a word of despair—but are instead a word of ringing faith—"Into your hands I commend my spirit" (Luke 23:46).

8

In the Face of Death, Lift High the Cross

Read
John 10:10; 14.

When the philosopher Henry David Thoreau was dying, a friend tried to turn his thoughts to the life beyond, only to receive the gentle rebuke, "One world at a time, brother . . . one world at a time." That rebuke expresses the thoughts of many when it comes to death. People see the subject of death as a dismal subject that they would prefer to have banished from their minds. "We need to deal only with the present," they say.

How long has it been since you have heard a sermon on death? It seems to be a subject that we don't want to talk about. Of course it is a subject that we know little about. We feel more comfortable talking about handling the death of family and friends. We talk very little about our own impending death.

Still, death is a fact of life, whether we choose to ignore it or not. Death stalks our streets like a grim specter without respect to persons. We may boast of our indifference to death, but underneath this nonchalant, devil-may-care attitude, a latent anxiety lurks. And little wonder. Paul was right: "If in this life only we have hoped in Christ, we are of all people most to be pitied" (I Corinthians 15:19).

Death was the subject of discussion in the Upper Room on the evening before Jesus' Crucifixion. The subject was heavy on the mind and heart of Jesus as well as his disciples. Not only the death of Jesus, but the disciples' death as well. One could sense it in the air. At that moment more than any other, death was near. From time to time Jesus had sought to prepare them, but they refused to hear him. Now, as they gathered for the last time, Jesus intended for them to hear. Jesus essentially said to them, "I do not want you to worry. Set your fears to rest. They are going to kill me. But I do not want you worrying about it. Because I will come to you, I will always be with you. Death is not final."

A few weeks earlier Jesus received the word that his friend Lazarus had died. He traveled to Bethany. Jesus said to Martha, "Your brother will rise again" (John 11:23). Martha missed the point. She said, "I know that he will rise again in the resurrection on the last day" (vs. 24). There was a vague belief in her day that at a great future time all the dead would rise. Jesus responded to her with an assurance that only Emmanuel, "God with us," could give: "I am the resurrection and the life. Those who believe in me, even though they die, will live, and everyone who lives and believes in me will never die" (vss. 25-26).

The discussion of death in the Upper Room is but an extension of the Bethany encounter. Jesus dealt directly with the issue of death. It teaches us that in the face of death, the death of someone dear to us or our own death, we can lift the cross high. In the Upper Room, Jesus declares that the Christian gospel speaks with assurance about life and death. It is concerned with this life, but only against the background of its impermanence. It cares profoundly for today because it cares still more profoundly about the last day, the climax of history, the consummation of all things in Christ.

Because of this assurance, there are some things we are able to understand about death.

DEATH IS EASIER TO ACCEPT WHEN WE RECOGNIZE IT AS A FACT OF LIFE

In *Poor Richard's Almanac*, Benjamin Franklin wrote, "Nothing in this world is certain but death and taxes." Normally, when Franklin is quoted, it is in reference to impending "taxes," not "death." We must live with taxation, and in some form or another we pay taxes each day. Death is different because we only die once. Depending on age and circumstance, many see death as something to dread.

There was a time when we believed that young people and children did not think about death. Today there is an alarming rate of suicide among children, adolescents, and young adults. There are many youth who do not think they will live to be adults. However, for the most part, the larger segment of the youth population believes itself to be invincible. Perhaps this is why children feel free to run and jump without thinking, and that is why teenagers race their cars thinking, "Hey, nothing's going to happen to me!"

As we get older, we begin to think about our own mortality. The body changes, we slow down, and more and more candles on the birthday cake document our progression in life. Little by little we may permit ourselves to think about the time when we will surely die.

There was a time when death was something our parents and grandparents faced with more frequency. The average life span was shorter then than now. Medical science was not as successful in saving human life. Infant mortality was higher. But there is another reason why death, or the reality of death, was closer then than perhaps it is now. There were fewer hospitals, and virtually no nursing homes. Sick and dying relatives more times than not died in their own homes. It was the custom, years ago, for the wake to be held in the family's living room since most undertakers did not yet offer the space in their funeral homes. There is another point that we need to remember. The reality of death was perhaps closer to most people years ago because cemeteries were on the church property. If you ever drive in the rural areas of America, take a close look at those small rural churches. More times than not the church is surrounded by a graveyard and every Sunday, when families went to church, they were again reminded of the reality of death as they passed the granite grave markers on their way to worship.

I am not implying that our ancestors permitted themselves to dwell on death in a morbid way, but death was a part of life for them. In many respects they were more fortunate than we are today, because their times and circumstances permitted them the opportunity to face openly and honestly the whole question of death. For them death was not something that was delayed for an indefinite period by miracle drugs. It wasn't something that happened in sterile hospitals and faraway nursing homes. This does not mean that they were immune from the pain and grief, nor were they stronger and more courageous than you and I at the time of death. I am suggesting only that they had more opportunities to face death with more honesty and openness than you and I do in our day. Today, more times than not, people ignore the inevitable—that all of us and all of those around us will someday die. So instead of denying the power of death, it is necessary for all of us, especially since we are Christian, to approach death in a realistic, compassionate, and biblical manner so that we will be better prepared to face our own deaths and the deaths of those we love.

DEATH IS EASIER TO ACCEPT WHEN WE LIVE LIFE TRIUMPHANTLY

I know a pastor who was diagnosed with terminal cancer. His physicians estimated that he would live six months. The lay leadership of the church, with every good intention, suggested that this man take more personal time for himself and family. They assured him that his salary would continue and his responsibilities would be covered by other staff members.

The word of his illness circulated rapidly through the church membership and the city. On the next Sunday, when he returned to his pulpit, the sanctuary was overflowing with worshipers. They came out of love and support for their pastor.

When it was time for the sermon, the pastor stood in the pulpit and declared, "For more than twenty-five years I have been your pastor. My physicians tell me that I have a very short time to live. During these years as your pastor, I have sought to teach you how to live. In the remaining months I have to live I intend to show you how to die."

He went about his pastoral responsibilities as usual. He preached each Sunday. Not until the very end, a few days before his death, did his illness prohibit him from performing his pastoral duties.

Someone has said, "We need to work each day as though we were never going to die, and we need to live each day as though it might be the last."

Death is not the worst thing that can happen to us. Often when someone we love is sick, our prayers are not always for God's will to be done. We insist that our will be done: "God heal my mother (child, wife, husband)." When that person dies, we claim God let us down, never realizing that death is God's perfect healing.

When my wife's mother was dying of lymphoma, she was hospitalized during her last days. Nan, having a healthy Christian understanding of life and death, insisted that there not be any life-support systems used to sustain her physical life. She said if her quality of life could not be maintained, she did not wish to remain alive on life-support systems. She said, "As a Christian, I am not afraid of dying. I am afraid of just being kept alive." We sat at her bedside during those last hours. On the night she died, her wonderful physician, himself a Christian, came in the early hours of the morning and sat with us until her death.

During the doctor's visit, we talked about Nan and her courage in the face of death. She was awake for much of the time. The doctor shared that when he sought admission to medical school, the dean asked him why he wanted to be a physician. He said, "So that I can prevent people from dying and cure disease." The dean replied, "If that is your purpose, you will be very frustrated. You cannot prevent death, only postpone it! And you cannot cure disease, only treat it." The doctor said the dean concluded: "Your only purpose as a physician is to help people have comfortable and quality lives while they have time on this earth."

To exist but not to really live is a senseless waste and one of life's starkest tragedies. Yet countless numbers of people find themselves doing precisely that. Like hamsters, running furiously on the revolving wheel in their cages, so many of us are caught in the frantic treadmill of life. We cover a lot of ground but really don't get anywhere.

There is a story of a wealthy man who died and, in accordance with his instructions, was to be buried in his gold Cadillac rather than an ordinary casket. As the Cadillac was being lowered into the huge grave, a bystander whispered in an awed voice, "Now, that's living!" Unfortunately, many people have been buried in high class who lived low lives. Jesus asked the question, "What does it profit them if they gain the whole world, but lose or forfeit themselves?" (Luke 9:25).

Lloyd Ogilvie tells of a father who knelt down beside his little boy's bed. It was time for prayers, hugs, and tender tucking. The little boy began his childhood prayer repeated so many times before: "Now I lay me down to sleep; I pray the Lord my soul to keep. If I should die before I wake, I pray the Lord my soul to take." On this night the words got mixed up and the child inadvertently spoke words of the greatest wisdom he would ever know. He prayed: "If I should wake before I die . . . . " Then he stopped in embarrassment and apologized, "Oh, Daddy, I got all mixed up." Wisely, his daddy responded with tender care. "Not at all, son; that is the first time that prayer was properly prayed. My deepest longing for you is that you may wake up before you die." The child drifted off to sleep, but the father turned the words over in his mind: "If I should wake before I die . . . . That's it," he exclaimed. "That is the promise of Jesus, 'I have come that you might have life and that you might have it in all its fullness.'"

There is a life that has meaning and does not wear out. It is a triumphant life. It is eternal life. Jesus has it; he gives it: "I came that they may have life, and have it abundantly" (John 10:10) What an offer—not a frustrated, bland existence, but fullness, completeness. Not a life shielded from disappointment or heartache, but a life that has eternal quality—an eternity that begins in the now and is forever.

Death is easier to accept when life, before death, is lived triumphantly.

DEATH IS EASIER TO ACCEPT WHEN WE BELIEVE THAT THERE IS MORE LIFE!

As I get older, I think of the passing of time and what Keats expressed in a sonnet. He said, "When I have fears that I may cease to be before my pen has glean'd my teeming brain." There is an incompleteness to what we know as life. We die without completion. There are so many more things to do, to create, so many ideas to entertain, relations to experience, things to hear and see and feel.

Chad Walsh understood this. He said, "The artist never quite captures the pigment of the mist in the mountain . . . the scientist sees the boundaries of his knowledge dissolving into a random jungle of equations. . . the musician never captures the sound, the tone, the perfect pitch." There is the human cry for more!

There is a steady force moving from what Emil Brunner called the "not yet" to the "now," and then relentlessly on to the "no longer." Surely it haunts each person during life. Meditate on it, and we know an inner clamor for a completion that life, as we know it, is powerless to satisfy.

Even though Jesus promised resurrection and eternal life, it is still hard to comprehend what life will be like after death. It seems so fantastic that it's hard to understand why the death of the body needs to interrupt the process of life and fill us with fear and anxiety.

Perhaps the most simple and deep-felt explanation of death and dying was offered by Dr. Elisabeth Kübler-Ross in her attempt to minister to a grieving family. She pointed out that death is very much like birth. For nine months, the unborn child is in the mother's womb. The baby knows no other existence. There is no light, no sound, no communication, and yet the unborn baby is content in its surroundings. It's warm, it's comfortable, it's safe. But then something strange happens that threatens the baby's simple existence. The walls around the baby expand and contract. The child is being pushed and forced out of the only existence it has ever known. It must be confusing and shocking; for one minute the unborn is at rest, but in a twinkling of an eye the baby's whole perspective is changed. Birth occurs. The baby leaves the womb and now enters a whole new world of sights and sounds, of taste and smells, a whole new world of new beginnings, new understandings, and new hopes.

Perhaps that is what Paul meant when he wrote in a letter to the Corinthians, "For now we see in a mirror, dimly, but then we will see face to face" (I Corinthians 13:12). So the death of the body is not the end but the beginning of a new stage in the ongoing process of life. And yet we fear death—the loss of control and the anxiety of the unknown.

In the Upper Room on that final night, Jesus proclaimed that there was "more." "I go to prepare a place for you, that where I am, there you may be." In that assurance we can live the life we know in its "fullness," and look with trust to the life we do not know.

Sharon Carr left a remarkable and enduring legacy. Stricken by a brain tumor in her youthful prime, she spent her few remaining years consumed in a struggle with death and an attempt to understand God's will.

Sharon had been pursuing a double major in English and religion at Emory University. She had a 3.9 grade point average. In May of 1989, Sharon, along with her family, sat in the front row at Emory University's commencement. Sharon sat in a wheelchair, and the dean came down to where she sat and presented her diploma. She graduated a Dean's Scholar.

Sharon established a close bond with her American Literature professor, Dr. Floyd Watkins. She sent him a collection of her poems and meditations. Dr. Watkins confessed that "most student poems are a burden in the life of a teacher of literature," but reluctantly he began to read them. "One poem drove me to the next," he said. "I found myself reading the best poetry I had ever read from a college student. The sensitivity, the poetic skill, the range of learning, the spiritual depth far excelled the work, I believed, of many accomplished poets."

Emory University's president, James Laney, read a few of Sharon's poems in a meeting of the Board of Trustees. Board members wept. All were deeply impressed by the poetic skill and depth of this nineteen-year-old.

In the year and a half of life that remained to her following graduation, Sharon worked with Dr. Watkins and others at Emory to prepare a book of her poems for publication. This was accomplished in 1991. The little volume of her poems and meditations, *Yet Life Was a Triumph*, reveals her joy in life, her trust in God, her fulfillment of spirit in the face of death, her confidence in eternal life.

Few people at the age of nineteen are put in the position of composing their own epitaph. It was read at her funeral.

I had to love today,
        because you couldn't promise me tomorrow.
    and my wealth is in the glimpse of the beyond
        that escapes the indifferent eye,
            flashing, twinkling in the tease of sunlight
            or the gray dewshine of raindrops . . .
    I had to hold tightly to purpose,

because you might not give me time for care-
lessness,
and lifeblood is too precious to spill on selfish
whim;
I had to cherish hope,
because you couldn't guarantee light
amid
despair, and I was tired of hurting . . . .
I am sustained by what I cannot see,
and reassured by a comforting grasp
that is all in all, ever powerful, ever good.
Because I was forced to live life boldly,
thankfully,
lovingly and
joyfully,
death is tender,
and life was a triumph.

Sharon Carr, in the face of death, lifted the cross high. She accepted death as a fact of life. She lived her life triumphantly, and now she abides in the nearer presence of God.

9

In the Face of Temptation, Lift High the Cross

**Read
Matthew 4:1-11;
Mark 15:29-32.**

We know about temptation! It is as old as Adam and Eve, and it is as current as "What shall I eat and drink for dinner?"

For the tempted, temptation is a fork in the road: the leading of God in one direction and the pull of the Tempter in the other. We must choose. Robert Frost wrote about forks in the road of life:

> I took the one less traveled by,
> and that has made all the difference.

Jesus said, "Enter through the narrow gate; for the gate is wide and the road is easy that leads to destruction, and there are many who take it. For the gate is narrow and the road is hard that leads to life, and there are few who find it" (Matthew 7:13-14). There is always a temptation that pulls us to the less than noble way. There is always a choice, but it is a chance to rise as much as it is a chance to fall.

Whatever temptation we face, there is always Jesus' example. Jesus was confronted with temptation throughout his earthly ministry. He spent forty days and nights in the wilderness in temptation as a means of testing his strength of faith and readiness for ministry. This testing experience was necessary to do battle with the one who held captive the people he came to redeem. His success or failure in his mission as the world's Redeemer was predicated on how he fared in this personal encounter. The will of Jesus was the focal point in the temptation experience. Would he render complete, unswerving obedience to the highest will of his heavenly Father? Or, under the most excruciating circumstances of human endurance, could he finally be broken down to compromise himself for the sake of survival? They say that every person has his or her price. Did Jesus have his? The resounding affirmation of the temptation episode proves, finally and for all time, that Jesus could not be bought for any price.

Simon Peter also tempted Jesus when Jesus began to make his plans to go to Jerusalem. Knowing that Jesus would suffer many things and be killed, Peter rebuked him saying, "God forbid it, Lord!" (Matthew 16:22). Jesus then turned to Peter and said, "Get behind me, Satan! You are a stumbling block to me; for you are setting your mind not on divine things but on human things" (vs. 23). And while Jesus was hanging on the cross, there were those who continued to taunt and tempt him to do and be less than God had called him to be. They said, "Let the Messiah, the King of Israel, come down from the cross now, so that we may see and believe" (Mark 15:32).

In spite of these temptations, Jesus remained faithful and obedient. Paul later wrote, "Let the same mind be in you that was in Christ Jesus, who, though he was in the form of God, did not regard equality with God as something to be exploited, but emptied himself, taking the form of a slave . . . humbled himself and became obedient to the point of death—even death on a cross" (Philippians 2:5-8).

We can take heart remembering that when we are in the struggle, Jesus is there struggling with us. In the face of temptation, the Christian lifts high the cross and is able to discover what Jesus understood about the Tempter, the temptation, and the tempted.

JESUS UNDERSTOOD THE REALITY OF THE TEMPTER

Evil is a grim, hideous reality. Why is it that so many of our sincerest plans for renewal are defaced and destroyed when their success seems inevitable? Why is it that society lapses so easily into strife and anarchy? Why are people so gullible to accept weird and noxious rumors and turn aside to lies? Why do we readily capitulate to greed, lust, anger, and pride, finding it far easier to surrender than to conquer? The New Testament answer to this question is unambiguous: "For our struggle is not against enemies of blood and flesh, but against the rulers, against the authorities, against the cosmic powers of this present darkness, against the spiritual forces of evil in the heavenly places" (Ephesians 6:12).

There is a cartoon in which one youngster asks another, "Do you believe in the devil?" The reply is, "Of course not, silly. It's like Santa Claus; it's only Daddy." Gerald Kennedy suggests that the Tempter's craftiest move ever has been to persuade Christians that the very idea of the existence of an evil force in the world was a bad dream that should never disturb their sleep.

C. S. Lewis wrote, "I know someone will ask me, 'Do you really mean, at this time of day, to reintroduce our old friend the devil . . . hoofs, horns, and all?'" To which he made answer: "What the time of day has to do with it, I don't know. And I am not particular about the hoofs and horns. But in other respects my answer is, 'Yes, I do.'"

Though ridding our minds of the ridiculous medieval caricature of the devil with horns and hooves could serve us well in reckoning with evil, we should not denounce the existence of an evil force in the world. In his book *Jesus, the Man Who Lives,* Malcolm Muggeridge has this to say about the Tempter: "Personally, I have found the Devil easier to believe in than God; for one thing, alas, I have had more to do with him. It seems to me quite extraordinary that anyone should have failed to notice, especially during the last half century, a diabolic presence in the world, pulling downwards as gravity does instead of pressing upwards as trees and plants do when they grow and reach so resolutely and beautifully after the light. Have we not seen the Devil's destructiveness making a bonfire of the past, present, and future in one mighty conflagration? Who can miss him in those blackest of all moments, when God seems to have disappeared, leaving the Devil to occupy an empty universe."

Our concern should not be with fashionable teaching but with sound, biblical teaching. The New Testament bears witness to the reality of Satan, giving him such names as the Deceiver, the Enemy, the Father of Lies, Tempter, the Ruler of the World, the Spirit that now works in the children of disobedience. The Evil One also goes about as a roaring lion seeking whom he may devour.

In Luke's Gospel it is recorded that Jesus said to his disciples, "I watched Satan fall from heaven like a flash of lightning" (Luke 10:18). Jesus did not regard the Tempter as superstitious nonsense, a hallucination induced by lack of food or the desert sun. His contest with him was real. The Tempter is real all right. All of us can testify to his mischievousness in our own lives.

Jesus Understood That Temptation Comes When We Are Conscious of Some Want in Our Lives

Students were preparing for a final exam in a college classroom. Before giving out the exam, the professor asked the students to spread out across the room, leaving a vacant seat between them and their neighbor student. She asked, "You know the 'good book' says that we should not 'yield to temptation.'" A student quipped, "What if we do not believe in the 'good book'?" The professor replied, "In that case, please sit two seats apart." No one is exempt from temptation. When something is lacking, we feel sorry for ourselves and seek to satisfy ourselves in ways and by means that may not be according to God's highest will for our lives. Loneliness, business pressures, exhaustion, insecurity, and depression are emotions and circumstances that

tempting situations

make us vulnerable to temptation. Jesus' temptations in the wilderness illustrate this well.

Jesus' first temptation was to turn stones into bread. Jesus was hungry. The Judean wilderness is an isolated and lonely place. When you are hungry and thirsty, as Jesus was, the wilderness is even more debilitating. I have spent some time there. The silence is overwhelming. The heat of the sun is unbearable during the day and the nights are freezing. At sunset, when the sun casts its warming glow across the Judean desert, the flat smooth stones of the wilderness turn golden brown. They remind you of fresh baked bread.

That was the setting when the Tempter came to Jesus and suggested that Jesus alleviate his hunger by turning the stones into bread. Eating food, however, was not what would do Jesus the most good at that moment. Jesus was hungry because he had chosen to fast. Jesus had entered the wilderness determined to attach himself inseparably to his real self, which is to God. The Tempter approached him and said, "If you are really the Son of God, and you are hungry, tell these stones to become bread. Don't be rigid about your determination to obey God. After all, you are hungry, and here is a way you, the Son of God, can satisfy your hunger pangs."

That is always the way it is: In a hundred different ways, every day, we become conscious of some want in our lives. We are tempted to compromise because of our need. We justify and excuse ourselves from moral responsibility. "Please excuse me from responsibility to live like a Christian today. My situation is unique." The appeal is to satisfy secular demands without the interference of the spiritual dimension.

For his second temptation, Jesus was led to the high
pinnacle of the temple. It was suggested that he might
cast himself down and win acceptance by such a dramatic arrival. Human nature is addicted to the spectacular. We have an instinctive love of the marvelous,
and curiosity about the supernatural. "Since you are the
Son of God, impress the people with a miracle," was the
appeal of the Tempter. It is the temptation to show off,
to be dramatic. Do you ever feel like that? We oftentimes go to radical lengths to get attention, to gain
recognition and acclaim.

In his third encounter with the Tempter, Jesus was
taken to a high mountain where there passed before
him, in a moment of time, all the kingdoms of this world
and the glory of them. The Tempter promised him, "All
these things will I give you, if you will fall down and
worship me." The temptation for Jesus was to gain the
crown without the cross—the temptation of power. It
was the same temptation of which he later warned his
disciples: "What will it profit them to gain the whole
world and forfeit their life?" (Mark 8:36).

Jesus' example in the face of temptation reminds us
that, in our struggle, he is struggling with us. Jesus was,
as the Scripture says, "in all points tempted as we are,"
and was faithful to the end. When we struggle, it is
ultimately with the issue of who we are as persons, as
Christians. That is always the temptation: to be deluded
into thinking that we are something less than God's.

JESUS UNDERSTOOD THAT THE TEMPTED NEED HELP

On the night before he was crucified, Jesus prayed
for the disciples who were gathered around him. He

was also praying for all the disciples down through the ages. He was praying for all of us who believe in him and trust him as Lord when he prayed: "I am not asking you to take them out of the world, but I ask you to protect them from the evil one. . . . Sanctify them in the truth; your word is truth" (John 17:15, 17). As he faced each temptation in the wilderness, Jesus warded off the Tempter with an appeal to scripture: "It is written." The scriptures were for Jesus and Paul as for us the sword of the Spirit. Jesus' devotion to the Word of God was undergirded by a life of prayer that continued through all temptations to the very last one: "If possible, let this cup pass from me."

Jesus not only prayed for us, but he also taught us to pray, "Lead us not into temptation." Paul assures us: "No testing has overtaken you that is not common to everyone. God is faithful, and he will not let you be tested beyond your strength, but with the testing he will also provide the way out so that you may be able to endure it" (I Corinthians 10:13). Do not think that your experience is unusual or exceptional.

The writer to the Hebrews encourages us: "We do not have a high priest who is unable to sympathize with our weaknesses, but we have one who in every respect has been tested as we are, yet without sin. Let us therefore approach the throne of grace with boldness, so that we may receive mercy and find grace to help in time of need" (Hebrews 4:15-16). In every time of need, in every testing, in every temptation, in every sin, and in every sorrow, Jesus is able to help those who are tempted because he won the victory there in the wilderness of Judea as well as through the thirty-three years of his life. "Because he himself was tested by what he suffered, he is able to help those who are being tested") (Hebrews 2:18).

In the wilderness of Judea, Jesus conquered the Tempter so that everyone defeated in the moral wilderness of our day might find in him the way out. Jesus knows the full fury of the struggle that people face in the world; where the victimized are struggling for justice, where the perverted and sex obsessed are looking for meaning in a world of dirty politics and vicious conflicts, of drug addiction and drunkenness, of broken homes and shattered lives. He does not condone the sin but seeks to help the sinner. He came not to condemn but to save. To the woman who was taken in adultery, he said, "Neither do I condemn you. Go your way, and from now on do not sin again" (John 8:11).

Jesus knows our world where respectable citizens wonder what advantage it is to stand up for what's right. He knows our world where moral standards are flouted and success seems to reward the unscrupulous.

Because Jesus conquered the Tempter, we do not need to experience defeat in our temptation experiences. As we let Christ be Lord of our lives, he leads us in continual conquest over sin and the Evil One. Be assured, "We are more than conquerors through him who loved us" (Romans 8:37).

10

When You Are Tempted to Run, Lift High the Cross

Read
Matthew 16:21-23;
26:47-56.

Camp Sumatanga, nestled in the mountains of North Alabama, is a special place for Christian youth. David Hutto, affectionately known as Uncle Dave, was the founder of Camp Sumatanga and served as the camp's first superintendent. He, along with a few visionaries, planned and developed the camp. Among the original landmarks in the camp is a lighted cross that stands on the mountaintop overlooking the camp and surrounding area. Visible for miles, the sight of this cross has inspired many over the years.

Uncle Dave accumulated many stories related to this cross. One he loved to share took place during a rare Alabama snowstorm. On the day following the storm, a well-dressed businessman appeared on Uncle Dave's doorstep. He asked if Uncle Dave would take him to the lighted cross. The roads were still iced over and since it was an eleven-mile trip up the mountain and over icy roads to the cross, Uncle Dave said that it would be several days before they could safely make the trip. The man insisted they go that day. Uncle Dave agreed after seeing how determined the man was to get to the cross.

They got into Uncle Dave's four-wheel-drive truck and drove to the cross. On the way, the man told Uncle Dave why it was so urgent that he go to the cross.

He explained that the night before, during the storm, he was flying a single-engine plane from Atlanta to Birmingham. The storm caused him to become disoriented and lose his bearings. He said he was blinded by freezing rain and snow, and the visibility was zero. Over his short-wave radio, he frantically called for assistance. "What is your position?" the voice on the radio inquired. He could not tell them. He then told Uncle Dave that, "at that moment, out of the blackness of the night there appeared a cross in the middle of the sky." He could not believe it. He thought he might be hallucinating. The cross became clearer. He radioed that he saw something that looked like a bright cross in the sky. Then the radio message came back on the air and gave him his position and directed him into the local airport in Gadsden, Alabama. Safe and on the ground, he inquired about the cross. The personnel at the little airport told him that he had seen the light of the cross located on the mountain at Sumatanga. He discovered that in addition to being a source of inspiration, the light of the cross is used by all major airlines as a directional marking for all flights between Birmingham and Atlanta.

The man proceeded to tell Uncle Dave that he had been unhappy and was running away from his wife and family, his job, and all his responsibilities. He told Uncle Dave his story of booze, burnout, and boredom. He felt that the only solution to his problem was either suicide or to run away as far as possible. That was the reason for his being in the plane on a stormy night. He said he believed that the cross was God's way of getting his attention. The lighted cross was the turning point in his decision to stop running and return to his family and responsibilities. He said that he made a vow to God to go to the site of the cross as soon as possible and offer a prayer of thanksgiving for life and for another chance.

When they reached the cross, the man went to the foot of the cross and knelt down and prayed. Uncle Dave went over and knelt with him, and they prayed together.

Later, as the stranger left, he said to Uncle Dave, "The cross helped me find my way to safety last night, but more important, I found my way back to God. I'll never be the same again."

A preacher friend of mine shared this story in a sermon one Sunday morning. Following the worship service, one of his lay leaders came up to him and said, "I am the man you were talking about in the sermon today." He went on to say, "Following my initial visit to the cross, I have, from time to time over the years, returned to the Sumatanga cross whenever I have been tempted to run. Each time, I get my bearings again and discover my way back home."

You are unusual indeed if you have never been tempted to run or escape from some task that needs to be done.

Jesus was tempted to run for the same reason. To deny this is to deny his humanity. He entered into a real struggle about going to Jerusalem. Galilee and familiar faces and surroundings pulled in one direction, and Jerusalem and the cross pulled in the other. Peter and the other disciples advised Jesus against going to Jerusalem. He labored over the choice of remaining in pleasant Galilee or accepting the responsibility of Jerusalem.

Jesus' prayer in Gethsemane, "Let this cup pass from me. Yet not my will, but thine," was an honest endeavor to know God's will. However, it was also an openness to entertain any way other than the cruel cross. Even Jesus was tempted to run.

That struggle continues in all our lives. When we are tempted to run from our own "Jerusalem," there is usually a more attractive "Galilee" inviting us.

There are many stories in the Bible of the noblest heroes struggling with the temptation to run. Not only were they tempted to run but they actually attempted to run.

Running manifests itself in different ways. For example, Jacob ran from Esau and obligation. Jonah ran from God's call to go to Nineveh. Elijah, exhausted and burned out, ran from Jezebel and responsibility. Peter proposed to remain on the Mount of Transfiguration and build three tabernacles. This was a form of running. In Caiaphas's courtyard, on the evening before Jesus' crucifixion, Peter not only was tempted but did run away.

Among the most interesting of the letters contained in our New Testament is a brief one written by the Apostle Paul to a young disciple named Titus. Apparently, Paul had assigned Titus to do missionary work on the island of Crete in the Mediterranean Sea.

Crete must have been a most undesirable place for a Christian, and there is every implication that Titus was miserable with his assignment. It is likely that he endured Crete for a period of time and then wrote to Paul, complaining of the hopelessness of the situation and asking to be relieved.

In his return letter to Titus, Paul seemed to confirm and justify any criticism that Titus may have made of Crete and the Cretans. He wrote, "It was one of them, their very own prophet, who said, 'Cretans are always liars, vicious brutes, lazy gluttons'" (Titus 1:12).

Now that would seem to most of us, as it must have seemed to Titus, reason enough to get out of Crete as soon as possible. But Paul had a word of advice for Titus, and perhaps for us, when he wrote that this was the very reason Titus could not run. Paul wrote to Titus, "I left you behind in Crete for this reason, so that you should put in order what remained to be done" (vs. 5).

"Crete" is fairly common in life. The place or situation may have a different name—Nineveh, Bethel, Jerusalem, or your hometown. The truth is that most of us have been there, others will be going there, and perhaps many of us are in "Crete" even now. Moreover, we are human enough that we are anxious to get out of there as soon as possible.

So what do we need to know whenever we are tempted to run?

The Temptation to Run Is Often Caused by Too Much Self-Concern

Biblical personalities were tempted to run away for the same reason we are: self-concern. Jacob, after betraying his father, Isaac, and his brother, Esau, found life unpleasant. When his life was threatened, he ran. Jonah could not imagine what life would be like in Nineveh. Elijah feared for his personal safety after Jezebel made her threat on his life. For Peter and the other disciples, they had their own agendas for Jesus. As for Titus, he just wasn't happy. He, like the others, had not learned the lesson that happiness in life is not determined by what is dealt to us but how we respond. And even in the life of Jesus there was self-concern. Jesus struggled with leaving his disciples to carry on his ministry when he was not certain that they were ready for such a task.

Helen Keller is a remarkable example of one who did not run away from what life dealt her. Her story is told in *The Miracle Worker*. Blind and deaf from early childhood, she might have retreated into self-pity. Instead, she created happiness where she was. She once said, "If I regarded my life from the point of view of the pessimist, I should be undone, I should seek in vain for the light that does not visit my eyes and the music that does not ring in my ears. I should beg day and night and never be satisfied. I should sit apart in awful solitude, a prey to fear and despair. But since I consider it a duty to myself and to others to be happy, I escape a misery worse than any physical deprivation."

It is important to learn that contentment or fulfillment is a by-product of living a faithful life. It is not something you seek or find as much as you create. If this is true, we might as well begin at Crete, Nineveh, or Bethel, as any place else.

Perhaps this is more difficult for us to learn than it was for any of the biblical personalities. I suppose no generation has been more self-oriented than our own. Self-interest has become a defining characteristic of our time. It has cost us the strength of character that is the fruit of such things as duty, discipline, integrity, and perseverance, and has rendered us incapable of the happiness which we value so highly. We have made personal contentment and comfort the ultimate objectives of life. We tend to measure everything by its contribution to our satisfaction. Even religious faith has fallen into this fallacy.

John Ruskin said, "We may always be sure, whatever we are doing, that we are not pleasing God if we are not happy ourselves." While there is an element of truth in this philosophy, there is also a great deal of danger in it. How many times have marriages been abandoned when the only reason given was that they were not happy or their needs were not being met? Other considerations such as marriage vows, the needs of the other partner, or the lives of children involved were overshadowed by one thing—self-concern.

THE TEMPTATION TO RUN IS OFTENTIMES SHORT-LIVED

Sometimes in the midst of some difficult situation or unpleasant experience it is hard for us to believe the circumstance will ever end.

An old preacher who had seen his share of hard experiences was asked by someone to name the most comforting text in the Bible. His questioner was surprised when the old preacher replied that he considered the most comforting words to be, "It came to pass."

It was pointed out that this was not a verse of Scripture, but only the beginning of one. "I know," said the preacher. "But those are the most comforting words in the Bible to me. It didn't come to stay; it came to pass."

The title of Antony Campolo's book, *It's Friday . . . But Sunday Is Coming!*, is based on a sermon preached by his pastor in Philadelphia. It was a sermon on hope and expectation. The pastor compared the troubles and storms of life to Good Friday. Just as the disciples were in deep despair on Friday, on Easter their darkness turned to light and their despair turned to hope. The Christian is one who, in the face of the Friday storm, is confident that God will calm the sea on Sunday.

Thomas Jefferson, the author of our nation's Declaration of Independence, once wrote his own revision of the Gospels. He was a great admirer of the teachings and sayings of Jesus. Jefferson was a good and moral man, guided by those teachings. However, he did not adhere to the supernatural content of the gospel story. Therefore, in his revision of the Gospels, Jefferson deleted all references to the supernatural. His account of the gospel ends with the Crucifixion and the burial of Jesus. The last words are: "They placed Jesus in the tomb and rolled a huge stone to cover the entrance."

We are thankful indeed that those are not the last words of the gospel story. Matthew records that "as the first day of the week was dawning, Mary Magdalene and the other Mary went to see the tomb. And suddenly there was a great earthquake; for an angel of the Lord, descending from heaven, came and rolled back the stone and sat on it." The angel said, "Do not be afraid; I know that you are looking for Jesus who was crucified. He is not here; for he has been raised" (Matthew 28:1*b*-2, 5-6*a*). Because of the resurrection, Matthew could later record the words of Jesus, who before his ascension promised, "I am with you always, to the end of the age" (Matthew 28:20*b*).

The Fridays of life come frequently for some. But when we learn to live in the light of the hope that Sunday is coming, then we can keep from despairing and running away. To some degree, Jacob and Jonah and Elijah came to discover this.

Even Titus found this to be true. He did not run. He remained in Crete and built the church. There must have been missionaries and Christian leaders from the church in Crete who went out all over the Greco-Roman world, for the church in the Western world is a legacy of the church at Crete. In spite of the temptation to run, Titus endured and helped great things happen in a place that he wanted to flee.

There is a chorus that Christians in Liberia love to sing. It addresses the issue of obedience to doing what God wants us to do. The words are, "I say yes, Lord, yes, to your will and to your way. I say yes, Lord, yes, I will answer and obey. When your spirit speaks to me, with my whole heart I agree . . . I say yes, Lord, yes."

THE TEMPTATION TO RUN IS ALWAYS A SIGN OF SPIRITUAL CRISIS IN OUR LIVES

Have you ever noticed that situations and circumstances from which we are tempted to run become the best places to permit ourselves to be found by God? Consider Jacob's experience at Bethel. If you have been to Bethel, you know that it is a dark and dismal place—the kind of place we would all want to flee. However, the writer of Genesis says that "Jacob woke from his sleep and said, 'Surely the LORD is in this place—and I did not know it!' And he was afraid, and said, 'How awesome is this place! This is none other than the house of God, and this is the gate of heaven'" (Genesis 28:16-17).

In the bleakness of what he called a dreadful place, Jacob found the presence of God. There he built an altar to God and called the place Bethel, which means "house of God." It is often true that the most difficult and trying experiences of our lives are potential "Bethels" for us.

Mark's Gospel summarizes Jesus' wilderness experience in a single sentence, saying, "He was in the wilderness forty days, tempted by Satan; and he was with the wild beasts; and the angels waited on him" (Mark 1:13). The report is brief, but something tremendous is shared in Mark's word that in the midst of our Lord's ordeal, "the angels ministered to him."

Often in the storms of life the angels minister to us. We find a closeness to God that we would never know if we were to run away.

Maurice Boyd tells the story of Hugh Redwood, a celebrated lay preacher in England who was in great demand as a speaker. During one period of his life, Redwood passed through a difficult time. He had some very hard decisions to make and wasn't sure what he should do. He was tempted to give it all up—to run. He asked God for guidance, but as sometimes happens, it seemed that no guidance was given. The heavens were silent.

One evening he went to have dinner with some friends before going on to address a large public gathering. When the meal was over his hostess suggested he go to the study, put his feet up, and relax beside the fire. Redwood was glad for a little peace and quiet, so that is what he did. He found, as promised, a fire in the grate. He sat down on the side of the bed and noticed that on the table beside the bed was a Bible. He picked it up and discovered that it was open to Psalm 59. He began to read, and when he came to the tenth verse he found these words underlined, "The God of my mercy shall prevent me" (KJV).

The word *prevent* as used in the King James Version of the Bible means "to go before." To prevent someone means to go before them. The text means, "The God of my mercy shall go before me." Someone had written a paraphrase of the text in the margin, and it found its way into Hugh Redwood's mind with such power that he never forgot it. The words in the margin were these, "My God, in His loving-kindness, shall meet me at every corner." For Hugh Redwood, that text was a light for his dark place. Later he made his hard decisions, and they proved to be wise ones. He did not run away but went on to accomplish great things and to live a useful and fulfilled life.

So many times the things we would sooner be rid of, or away from, are God's greatest opportunities. If we yield to the temptation to run, we breach the trust God has given us and the hope God has placed in us.

Think, for a moment, of the difference that truth could make if whenever you find yourself in distressing circumstances and want to run away, when you are anxious, when your heart is terrified at what tomorrow will bring, you were to say to yourself, "My God, in his loving-kindness, shall meet me at every corner." Every life has its dark moments and its corners. We cannot see around them, and because we don't know what is waiting for us, we are apprehensive. We are not sure what demands will be made on our courage or fortitude. And so we are afraid and are tempted to run.

But suppose we were to say and to keep on saying to ourselves, "God is already there! Before I enter this experience of anxiety or weakness, God is already present strengthening me for it and meeting me in it." Wouldn't that affirmation strengthen our confidence and renew our courage?

This was the experience of Bishop Arthur Kulah of Liberia, a courageous individual with a compassion for the plight of his people in the midst of war and poverty. For more than five years Kulah has sought to be the peacemaker. He has survived threats to do him bodily harm or take his life. At times he has been forced into hiding. He shared with me the mental anguish he experienced while hiding from government forces at times and rebel forces at other times.

Near the end of President Doe's regime, Kulah had been forced into an extensive period of hiding. His hiding place was always among his church people in the villages. Bishop Kulah did not cease his peace efforts and his strong opposition to the oppressive Doe regime, even though he was in hiding. During this time Doe announced a generous reward for anyone who would kill Kulah.

Bishop Kulah reached the point where he said enough was enough. He was convinced that God did not want him to spend his days mulling around in the villages. So he decided that on the next morning he would walk, alone, from the village to the mission compound. It was a trip of more than ten miles on the busiest highway in Liberia. The route was covered with more than one hundred military checkpoints located every five hundred feet. Normally, the checkpoints were occupied with six to ten Doe soldiers.

Bishop Kulah made it known that he was going to make the trip and the word went before him that he was coming. Before embarking on his walk he met with the church members and they prayed. He said that they prayed not only for safety and protection, but also for God's will to be done. Their prayer was that their bishop would have continued courage to be faithful and obedient to God.

As he started out he expected to be killed. He said, "I constantly repeated the words of Jesus, 'Lo I am with you . . . always.'" An interesting thing happened when he reached the first checkpoint. There was no sign of life. No one was on the street. Five hundred feet down the road was the next checkpoint. The same thing. The trip took him by the major army barracks. No one was at the gate. He traveled, walking in the middle of the highway, the entire ten miles to the mission compound without seeing a single soldier.

Bishop Kulah refers to the experience as his "Miracle Walk." He took me over the route. We were stopped at the many checkpoints, endured the many indignities of meaningless questions, and drove by the army barracks. We encountered hundreds of soldiers armed with automatic weapons. When I reflect on the bishop's walk, it was a "miracle." I will never forget his words, "It was like God was going before me—making me a path. It was like God's promise to Isaiah: 'When you pass through the waters, I will be with you.' And he was."

When you are tempted to run—lift high the cross! Remind yourself that the temptation to run oftentimes occurs when we are preoccupied with our own concerns, the temptation to run is often short-lived, and that it is in the midst of such temptation that we can find a renewed sense of God's presence in our lives.

11

When You Are Tempted to Just Go Along, Lift High the Cross

Read
John 12:12-13,
23-26;
Romans 12:2.

I once heard of an interesting experiment in the psychology department of a major midwestern university. Twelve persons were gathered in a room. Some were graduate students; others were members of the faculty and the administration. Each person was given a set of earphones. Seated in their separate places, they were to listen for a buzzer. When it sounded, they were to report orally the number of sounds they heard.

A faculty member from the sociology department was seated in the twelfth chair. Being the university type, he was mildly amused at the elementary nature of the assignment. The first series of sounds was heard, and he counted patiently eighteen sounds. The first person was asked to report the number of sounds heard, and she said sixteen. The professor smiled at the thought of the woman not being able to count to eighteen accurately. But the next person in the circle was asked, and he said he heard sixteen sounds. Person number three said the same. And on it went through the first eleven persons; each said that sixteen sounds were heard. So the professor, thinking that he perhaps had erred while he counted, finished up the tally by reporting sixteen sounds.

The same process was repeated. This time the professor counted nine. During the second round all claimed to have heard eleven sounds. When it came time for the professor to report, he sighed with resignation and said "eleven."

In succeeding rounds, the numbers varied wildly. Sometimes they were off as much as half the number. But each time the sociology professor reported hearing whatever the first eleven reported. And before the experiment was over, he simply stopped counting. "It is clear that they know something I don't," he said to himself. "The dummies all report what they heard before they get to me. By being last, I can just let them figure it out and report whatever they say since they seem to know."

You doubtless already know what he should have known. There were not twelve subjects in the experiment; there was only one. And the good professor was it. The others were involved in the experiment and were told to invent numbers that were progressively off the mark. They were waiting to see just how ridiculous their answers would have to be to goad the stalwart subject to produce a contrary opinion.

There is an elaborate network of voices arrayed about us prompting us on the answers to the questions of life. Indeed, it goes farther than that. The network of voices even suggests to us that, in a world where some of us have more than we need and others lack enough merely to survive, we ought to be asking how we can get more for ourselves. In a world where people want desperately to be able to form lasting community, we are taught to look out for number one. We go to church, having heard the numbers called all week, to restore ourselves to our rightful mind. We remind ourselves that life oriented around loyalty to the One to whom final loyalty is justly due, is life that is transformed because its very mind is renewed. "If anyone is in Christ, he is a new creation; the old has passed away, behold, the new has come."

The psychology experiment may only be mildly embarrassing, but its implications are devastating. For we show far more willingness than we would like to think to call out the answers that the world has proclaimed. In too many cases we have conformed to the world.

It is an awesome thing to be faced with difficult circumstances. A more fearful development is to be trapped or enslaved in a mentality that calls for us to simply conform our thinking to what is around us.

Christians have forever been plagued with the temptation to do the expedient. Afraid of "making waves," being unpopular, or losing money, status, or power, we often believe the best way to get along is to go along.

The temptation to "go along," to accommodate a sinful society, is invariably disastrous. The community of believers fails to preserve its distinctive identity as the Body of Christ, and the penetrating challenge and redemptive power of the gospel is blunted. Individual believers lose that spiritual "edge," and there is nothing about our lives or behavior to remind others that God was in Christ reconciling the world to himself.

How many spiritual casualties owe their condition of debility to an irresponsible and undisciplined flirting with the world? The most painful sentence Paul had to write about a fellow worker was, "Demas, in love with this present world, has deserted me."

To be set free from the pressures to conform to the society around us means that we can speak the truth in love and not fear the consequences. It means that we no longer send the sails up to see which way the present winds of opinion are blowing before we take a stand. It means we are free from the pressure of being squeezed into the mold of the world and its opinion. We are able to speak the truth in clarity and love.

Jesus never just "went along." Jesus, the nonconformist, always did the unexpected, the unconventional, the unpredictable. This was disconcerting to both his enemies and his followers.

He forced would-be followers to get outside themselves and seek to do their best to follow and to understand, or he forced them to take refuge behind their defenses of indifference or outright animosity.

It is amazing that the disciples could be with Jesus daily and yet often miss his spirit. Mark recorded one of these moments when people were "bringing little children to him in order that he might touch them" (Mark 10:13). The disciples rebuked Jesus for doing this because children were understood to be of lesser value in their society. Jesus was indignant. If we wish to know what things Jesus cared deeply about, one sure clue is to be found in the things that roused his indignation. Here he is indignant because of the officious blindness that tried to keep children away from his blessing—the spiritual obtuseness that attempted to block their way. Jesus said, "Do not hinder the little children." They have a place. It is difficult today, living in our Western culture where children are given a significant place, to imagine a time when they were as chattel. Jesus confronted that system.

Jesus also went counter to the culture by inviting women—also second-class citizens—to be disciples. In his account of the gospel, John shares the experience of Jesus and the disciples when they came to a city in Samaria called Sychar. Jacob's well was there, and John writes, "Jesus, tired out by his journey, was sitting by the well. It was about noon. A Samaritan woman came to draw water, and Jesus said to her, 'Give me a drink.' (His disciples had gone to the city to buy food.) The Samaritan woman said to him, 'How is it that you, a Jew, ask a drink of me, a woman of Samaria?'" (John 4:6-9).

What followed was one of the most memorable exchanges recorded in the New Testament. When the disciples returned from the city, "They were astonished that [Jesus] was speaking with a woman" (John 4:27). They marveled because Jesus was going "against the grain" of what was the accepted behavior of a Jewish rabbi. It was Jesus who broke tradition and gave a woman a prominent place. He saw the possibilities and values in women just as he did in men. It was Christ who lifted woman into equality with man. That was a real strain on the disciples.

One day the religious leaders of the community, all men, had trapped a prostitute. In their day, prostitution was so loathsome that it was beyond contempt. But there was something incongruous about this picture. They stood there excitedly anticipating a bloody end for this scarlet woman who, according to Mosaic law, must now be stoned to death. They couldn't wait to begin the dirty business. However, in order to play the cat and mouse game with her, they brought the woman before Jesus and asked, "Is there any other alternative but to keep the law of Moses, and stone her to death?"

Surely, they expected Jesus to yield at that point. How would he dare challenge the existing code of conduct? But nonconformist that Jesus was, he wrote in the sand with his finger. Then, he said to them, "Let anyone among you who is without sin be the first to throw a stone at her" (John 8:7).

It must have been almost ludicrous, Jesus continuing to write in the sand with his finger and the elders leaving one by one, dropping their stones and making themselves walk away with dignity while in their hearts they were running scared. The woman sits sobbing before him, expecting her just condemnation from the lips of this good man. But his words are unexpected: "Is there no one left to condemn you?" "No sir," she replies. "Well, I do not condemn you either. You may leave, but do not sin again."

On another occasion, a little man climbed into a tree to hear Jesus preach. He was the kind of person no one wanted to waste time with because he was a tax collector. Tax collectors were deeply disliked, and no self-respecting person had anything to do with them.

Jesus saw him straining to hear the word, looking for some hopeful sign, and ready to break out of his role if only someone gave him the least encouragement. The tax collector hated himself for what he was and for the role he had to play. If only somewhere he could know love instead of hate. Then Jesus looked up in his direction. The look was followed by inviting words: "Zacchaeus, hurry and come down; for I must stay at your house today" (Luke 19:5).

Unthinkable! Jesus, the respected teacher, breaking the unwritten rules that said that the only way to handle these people is to hate and avoid them. The Gospel narrative describes the mood: "All who saw it began to grumble" (Luke 19:7). They were the conformists. They complained about the fact that Jesus was going to be a guest at the home of a sinner. Jesus told Zacchaeus, "I'm coming." Jesus knew the terrible wants in the life of that man. He knew what lay imprisoned behind the crushed exterior. The itinerant teacher came and changed the life of Zacchaeus. We don't know what happened, but we do know that Zacchaeus found his better self. An unconventional man had taken the time to love, and in the process, a societal reprobate became a transformed person.

That is the way it was throughout Jesus' ministry. He was Christ, the nonconformist, doing the unpredictable thing, the strange thing, and always the right thing—not unreasonableness in order to gain his own way, not destroying old values, but fulfilling them, enriching them, and giving them a new dimension. Jesus was not so much against, as he was for something better. He said, "I have not come to destroy the law, but to fulfill it." His mission was not so much to throw out sacred traditions, but to make them meaningful. Jesus always added the positive factor. He always introduced us to something better, more meaningful, and more significant.

Jesus' ideas regarding messiahship were the ideas of one who was emancipated from the temptation to go along. They went counter to those held by his closest disciples as well as the religious leaders of his day. Jesus spelled out his ideas about messiahship in John 12:23-26. These three simple ideas have profound implications for us. They are variations of the central truth that is the heart of the Christian faith: that of denying oneself and lifting high the cross.

Only by Death Comes Life

Now as in Jesus' day, people want to live many years. The idea that life comes only by death is absurd! Few of us welcome the death of our bodies. Yet Jesus said we are like the grain of wheat. "Unless a grain of wheat falls into the earth and dies, it remains just a single grain; but if it dies, it bears much fruit" (John 12:24). Then he said, "Those who love their life will lose it, and those who hate their life in this world will keep it for eternal life" (John 12:25). We understand the seed in the ground portion of the passage, but we, along with his disciples, stumbled when Jesus says we are like that. The disciples also stumbled when Jesus said he was like that. None of his hearers could abide such a statement. "What is this—the messiah must die to live? What kind of nonsense is that?"

We must never forget what history tells us about the church. The expression "The blood of the martyrs is the seed of the church" is accurate. The church grew because of the martyrdom of its apostles and leaders down across the first centuries. It has thrived and continues to do so, wherever there has been acceptance of demanded sacrifice of life and limb for the faith. Because they died, the church became the "living church." William Barclay wrote in his *Bible Commentary,* "By the loyalty which was true to death, there have been preserved and born the most precious things which humanity possesses." Jesus set the pattern—the cross! When we are tempted to do less, we are to lift high the cross.

ONLY BY SPENDING LIFE DO WE RETAIN IT

Try that theory in economics and you will soon go broke. Yet Jesus said that is what must happen to the Christian life. The person who is motivated by selfishness and the desire for security loves this life more than anything else. Jesus insisted that the person who hoards his life will lose it in the end.

Think what this world would be like if it had not been for the nonconformists, those persons who could forget their personal welfare, their own safety, their own security, and their own selfish gain and advancement. Our world owes much to persons who recklessly spent their strength and gave themselves to God and to others.

ONLY BY SERVICE COMES GREATNESS

Jesus said, "Whoever serves me must follow me, and where I am, there will my servant be also. Whoever serves me, the Father will honor" (John 12:26). We speak of Jesus as the one for others and believe that his example should be followed by all who name his name.

Yet how much of our lives are really devoted to this proposition? How much of our time do we devote to serving God and others? The truth is—very little. Jesus tried, time and time again, to get across to his disciples that their ministry was for others. Jesus indicated that in serving others his followers were serving him. He reminded them that if they sought to be great they would need to humble themselves and lift high the cross.

On the night before the crucifixion, while they were gathered in the Upper Room, Jesus demonstrated, once and for all, the life of service he demanded of those who would follow him. He took a pitcher of water and a basin; he girded himself with a towel and went to each disciple and washed his feet. He asked them, "Do you know what I have done to you? . . . I have set you an example [to wash one another's feet]" (John 13:12-15).

We can be sure that in this world, where the pressure is to be squeezed into the mold of the world, Christ, the nonconformist, makes his appeal to the conscience of everyone. In our society, a Christian is generally thought to be the example of conventional morality. The Christian is the sound and safe member of the community. While these are certainly commendable characteristics, should a Christian be safe and sound in a world of horror and want? In a world of suffering and injustice, can a Christian be content with being respectable? I think not. Should a Christian not be identified with the oppressed? Is it possible that this is what, in part, it means to be a Christian? We are called to identify with the redemptive purposes of God. This is ultimately what it means to lift high the cross.

Christ, the unconventional, sought only the more excellent way. He asks the same of us. Paul stated it clearly when he wrote, "Do not be conformed to this world, but be transformed by the renewing of your minds, so that you may discern what is the will of God—what is good and acceptable and perfect" (Romans 12:2).

I have a friend who has a gift shop on the Via Doloroso in Jerusalem. Her name is Frieda Hannah. Frieda is a Palestinian Christian. She makes beautiful embroidery and cross-stitch work. Her specialties are altar paraments, clergy stoles, and Bible markers. I have purchased many over the years and she has, out of our friendship, given me some items that I cherish. She is a very frail woman. She has been in business at the same spot, the sixth station of the cross, for more than thirty years. Her eyes are beginning to fail her. She must wear thick glasses.

If you go by her shop you will see her smiling and greeting the tourists. She has made friends with thousands. A teacher friend said that one day he was in her shop with a group of students. Another large group of pilgrims from America were in the shop. They all had their Bibles under their arms and crosses hanging from their necks. They were pushing and shoving, demanding to be waited on. A group of little Palestinian beggars had followed the group into the shop asking for money. These "Christian" tourists were indignant. My friend said they made comments like, "Get these dirty kids out of here." Or, "Why don't they stay in Jordan where they belong?" Frieda overheard these remarks. My friend was embarrassed and apologized for his fellow Americans, even though he did not even know them. Frieda's response was, "Oh, that is all right. I learned a long time ago that many of those who insist on taking the Bible literally don't take it seriously."

Frieda certainly takes the Bible seriously. During the last thirty years, using the earnings from her little shop, she has given over 1,000 Palestinian youth a higher education in North America or Europe. She has built and supported the operation of three medical clinics in the West Bank. She has built and operates two orphanages. There is no way of determining the good that this Christian woman has done over the years.

Of course she is a modest person. She is always embarrassed to talk about what she does. When asked on one occasion where she gets the energy and determination, she responded, "God did not place me in this world just to take up space. It is not enough just to go along. God wants me to make a difference where I can."

When you are tempted to conform, remember Frieda, but more than that, remember Jesus, and lift high the cross.